on Alcantara • Karen Alexander • Victor Alfaro • Linda Allard • Jeanne A

nie August • Dominick Avellino • Max Azria • Yigal Azrouel • Mark Badgley • Kara Varian Ba

tta Bauer • Bradley Bayou • Geoffrey Beene • Alvin Bell • Jacques Bellini • Richard Bengtsson • Russell Bennett • Diane

Blass • Sherrie Bloom • Franklin Bober • Kenneth Bonavitacola • Sully Bonnelly • Jeannene Booher • Ole Bordon • Marc

Browne • Brian Bubb • Dana Buchman • Jason Bunin • Stephen Burrows • Anthony Camargo • David Cameron • Patti

Pierre (Pierrot) Carrilero • Liliana Casaba • Allen Case • Oleg Cassini • Edmundo Castillo • Salvatore Cesarani • Julie

vid Chu • Eva Chun • Doo-Ri Chung • Liz Claiborne • Patricia Clyne • Carol Cohen • David Cohen • Meg Cohen • Peter

k • Bern Conrad • Kathryn Conover • Martin Cooper • Jo Copeland • Maria Cornejo • Andrew Corrigan • Esteban

Cullinane • Angela Cummings • Eloise Curtis • Lilly Daché • Sandy Dalal • James Daugherty • Robert Danes • David

ela Dennis • Jane Derby • Giorgio di Sant'Angelo • Kathryn Dianos • Stephen DiGeronimo • Piero Dimitri • Dominic

Sam Edelman • Warren Edwards • Lola Ehrlich • Florence Eiseman • Mark Eisen • Perry Ellis • Melinda Eng • Olga

chi • Joseph Famolare • Gaetano Fazio • Jay Feinberg • Han Feng • Andrew Fezza • Alfred Fiandaca • Patricia Ficalora

ncis • Isaac Franco • Robert Freda • R. Scott French • Carolee Friedlander • James Galanos • Nancy Ganz • Annemarie

• Geoffrey Gertz • Mossimo Giannulli • Nicholas Graham • Marc Grant • Cindy Greene • Henry Grethel • George Gublo

glas Hannan • Cathy Hardwick • John Hardy • Karen Harman • Dean Harris • Johnson Hartig • Sylvia Heisel • Nancy

Nick Hilton • Kazuyoshi Hino • Catherine Hipp • Carole Hochman • Carole Hom • Donald Hopson • Chuck Howard

• Alexander Jordan • Andrea Jovine • Victor Jovis • Alexander Julian • Gemma Kahng • Bill Kaiserman • Kalinka • Norma

aye • Kazuko • Rod Keenan • Randy Kemper • Pat Kerr • David Kidd • Barry Kieselstein-Cord • Bud Kilpatrick • Eugenia

Michael Kors • Reed Krakoff • Michel Kramer • Regina Kravitz • Devi Kroell • Flora Kung • Blake Kuwahara • Steven

Jay Lane • Helmut Lang • Liz Lange • Byron Lars • Hubert Latimer • Ralph Lauren • Helen Lazar • Jack Lazar • Susan

ne • Brett Lewis • Marilyn Lewis • Monique Lhuillier • Antoinette Linn • Deanna Littell • Elizabeth Locke • Jean Louis

urice Malone • Colette Malouf • Isaac Manevitz • Robert Marc • Mary Jane Marcasiano • Georges Marciano • Stanley

rie McCarthy • Jessica McClintock • Jack McCollough • Mary McFadden • Marlo McGriff • Maxime McKendry • Mark

ael • Carlos Miele • E. Jerrold Miller • Glen Miller • Nicole Miller • James Mischka • Richard Mishaan • Isaac Mizrahi

Morrison • Rebecca Moses • Kathy Moskal • Matt Murphy • Anthony Muto • Morton Myles • George Nardiello • Leo

ilsson • Albert Nipon • Pearl Nipon • Roland Nivelais • Danny Noble • Vanessa Noel • Charles Nolan • Norman Norell

• Marie-Anne Oudejans • Rick Owens • Yonson Pak • Patricia Pastor • Mollie Pamis • Marcia Patmos • Edward Pavlick

Platt • Alexandre Plokhov • Carmelo Pomodoro • Regina Porter • Zac Posen • Anna Maximilian Potok • Gene Pressman

ina Riedel • Robert Riley • Sara Ripault • Judith Ripka • Bill Robinson • Patrick Robinson • Shannon Rodgers • David

• Ivy Ross • Martin Ross • Christian Roth • Christian Francis Roth • Cynthia Rowley • Ralph Rucci • Sabato Russo

Sandler • Angel Sanchez • Fernando Sanchez • Lauren Sara • Behnaz Sarafpour • Fernando Sarmi • Janis Savitt • Don

n • Christopher Serluco • Michael Seroy • Ronaldus Shamask • George Sharp • Marcia Sherrill • Alexander Shields • Sam

Michael Simon • Don Simonelli • George Simonton • Adele Simpson • Pamela Skaist-Levy • Stella Sloat • Eric Smith

Michael Spaulding • Peter Speliopoulos • Laurie Stark • Richard Stark • George Stavropoulos • Carole Stein • Cynthia

ren Suen-Cooper • Anna Sui • Charles Suppon • Gene Sylbert • Viola Sylbert • Robert Tagliapietra • Elie Tahari • Richard

n • Ben Thylan • Bill Tice • Frank Tignino • Monika Tilley• Zang Toi • Isabel Toledo • Julian Tomchin • Susie Tompkins

Tyler • Patricia Underwood • Kay Unger • German Valdi • Tony Valentine • Carmen Marc Valvo • Koos van den Akker

urstenberg • Patricia von Musulin • Diane Vreeland • Ilie Wacs • Tom Walko • Norma Walters • Vera Wang • Gale Warren

Whitledge • Edward Wilkerson • Arthur Williams • Harriet Winter • Judith Wister • Nancy White • Jenny Bell Whyte

er Wrigley • Gerard Yosca • David Yurman • Gabriella Zanzani • Katrin Zimmermann • ltalo Zucchelli • Ren Zuckerman

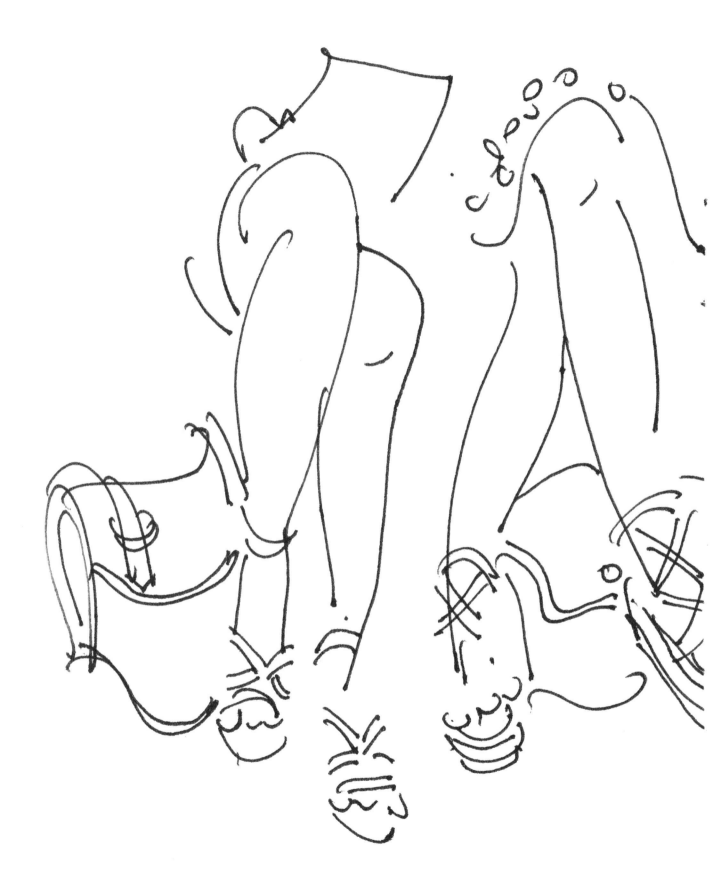

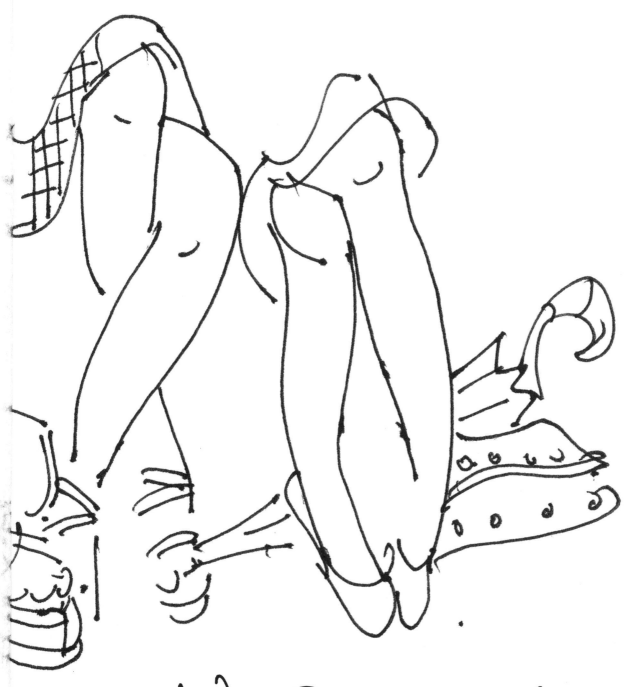

Un Cross Your legs

UNCROSS YOUR LEGS
A LIFE IN FASHION

STAN HERMAN

POINTED LEAF PRESS

HERMAN

Stan H...

by
Fashion...

A DIVISION OF HAR...

NAME _____

wman

FOR

ine®

SCHAFFNER & MARX

®

PART I: THE SET UP

It has been surprisingly easy to remember the building blocks of my early life. I do wonder how accurate I've been, but there are few left to challenge me.

THE BEGINNING

It has taken me 90 years to sit down and uncross my legs, to finally loosen the reins and write about my life. I have been writing stories for over 30 years, just after my lover Gene Horowitz died, encouraged by my friends and family who felt I had a story to tell. Reading Jan Morris' diary, *In My Mind's Eye*, written in her 92nd year, finally gave me the courage to complete the recipe of my life, take all of those ingredients to create my very own strawberry shortcake and share it with my world.

"Uncross your legs," just as the lights go down or up according to the venue. There is almost always a chorus of voices from the sardine-crammed photographers at the end of the runway. "Uncross your legs!" No one is immune. Those in the front row quickly unfold those well-heeled gams so that the sightlines are clear and the show can begin.

In the beginning, I was a breach baby. I used to think that is why I'm gay. I don't know how I got the idea, but that and the fact that I was also colicky, and would fall asleep only on my father's chest the first six months of my life, sealed the deal. These days people talk about a gay gene. Makes sense to me. These days people talk a lot about their sexual preference, not about which end saw the light of day first.

I was 6 pounds 3 ounces on the scales at Brooklyn Jewish Hospital, born to a mother who was told she should not have children. Having been born with a heart murmur, she developed a heart-lining infection, and unfortunately her system could not take the sulfur treatments available. Penicillin had not yet been invented. So her life was short, just 36 years. I was 12 when she died, almost ready to wrap myself in a tallis and bend to the Torah to 'become a man,' a man without a mother. *Die Mutter*, Siegfried sings to some of the most sublime music ever written.

I did not grow up in Brooklyn, but Brooklyn shaped my growing up. The Tannenbaum family of Brownsville and Pitkin Avenue, and the leafy streets of Strauss Street were like a Viennese waltz to me—the orchestral sounds of your next door neighbor's snoring, sharing attached front porch conversations, snapping iggies against the side of the house, always looking forward to the long trip from New Jersey in our oversized Nash sedan, motor off while we sailed the choppy Hudson River ride to Manhattan, and marveled at the dizzying height of the Williamsburg Bridge arching over the East River.

My younger brother Harvey had a special place in the back with me. He always slept in a makeshift hammock made from a baby blanket and tied to the windows with backyard rope. My job was to keep him quiet by rocking him to sleep to keep the peace. The distance from the Herman household in New Jersey to the Tannenbaum world in Brooklyn was short—the lifestyle, continents apart.

The Tannenbaums were a large family, six daughters and two sons. The younger son, David, known as Sonny to his family, became my surrogate father. He entered my life early and didn't leave until his death 82 years later. My apartment in New York is a museum of photographs. One of those well-framed pictures is Sonny in his shiny youth. He is wearing a beautifully cut double-breasted jacket framing his white flannel pleated pants. He was a beauty. I often found myself looking at him with exotic intensity. There is a snapshot in my head of his penis. I remember seeing it when I visited him during World War II while he was stationed in Pittsburgh. I don't remember how it happened, but looking back, it had to have been one of the first recognizable stirrings I had for my own sex, pre-puberty.

The sisters Tannenbaum would be a great vaudeville opening act. Except for my mother and her older sister Jean, who threw herself under a subway three months before I was born, they all lived long lives. I take that back, the youngest sister and my favorite, Esther, made it to her early 50s before leukemia swallowed that glowing personality. I imagine the opening act would have been Dorothy, Rose, and Bertha singing *Red Sails in the Sunset*, done to the Andrews Sisters beat entertaining the troops from World War II. To this day, it is still one of my favorite songs.

When looking back, I tend to romanticize the moment. I am sure those leafy streets have many dark shadows, the wailing vendor and his pushcart more *Mahogany* than *Fledermaus*, and those three sisters probably had no rhythm. That time, over 80 years ago in the heart of Brooklyn, still shimmers with intensity in my mind. I did grow up in Passaic, New Jersey, a midsize town just 12 miles west of the Hudson River, a town laid out very much like the European villages that were small in size, with a thriving business center and a railroad slashing its Main Street in two. It was a watering stop for trains on the Erie railroad inching their way to the heartland, Pittsburgh, Cleveland, and Chicago. It was a river town with waters that enticed large fabric mills like Botany and Forstman Mills to settle into its armpits; something about the softness in the water that elevated fabric dying to an art form.

You could easily stay in town without venturing to New York. There were five movie theaters, one of them offering big band entertainment: Tommy Dorsey, Harry James, and a very young Frank Sinatra in person. There were two white table-clothed restaurants—one Chinese, the other known appropriately as the Ritz, frequented by most of the Jews in town. There were enough church spires to pierce the heavens with their prayers to make their congregations comfortable. The Jews lived in Passaic Park where the trees were taller and the butcher charged twice the amount to carve the kosher meat. The Jewish population was almost a third of the total and large enough to become a force in the city politic. Passaic actually lulled you with its small town pleasantness and, yet, for me, there was always that trip to Brooklyn, bypassing Manhattan island, that would someday be my real home.

The Hermans were also a large family—six sons and one daughter. Their presence in the town did not go unnoticed. My grandmother and grandfather, a Jewish version of the famous Grant Woods couple, always faced the camera in their pictures with that stony expression that gives nothing away and still keeps you interested. She was a tiny

lady from head to toe; only her thick ankles were a giveaway to harder times. He had the posture of an academic who became a substitute teacher. A good-looking man with little character in his face, typical of the misplaced European intellectual who came from Jewish academia and ended up a furrier. He made some of the ugliest Peter Pan-collared seal coats I would ever see. I always picture him sitting, arms crossed in his little storefront immediately across the street from his son's luxurious silk shop, a store that captured the patronage of home sewers from every corner of northern Jersey, the shop that more than anything in my young life prepared me for my eventual life in fashion. All of those bolts of woollens and cottons, rayons and silk, not a poly in sight, and in one corner an elaborate pattern department, a battery of books from *Simplicity* to *Vogue* to seduce you toward your sewing machine. I loved that corner. I often worked there assisting women in their choices, trying to move them from *McCall's* to *Vogue*, *Advance* to *Simplicity*.

Grandma Herman would be perched on a high stool next to the cash register lording it over the satin lining section, counting and recounting the sales slips. Not a penny got by her. My grandpa sat on his low stools in a store across the street, surrounded by all those slaughtered seals. Years later, I walked away from a fur contract faced by a battery of fox pelts hanging in the back rooms of my first and only fur licensee.

Over these many years, I have faced off with the slaughter of animals, especially as President of the CFDA, trying to keep my personal feelings in check. I've sat through shows, been splattered with red paint, escorted Elsa Klensch, the woman who brought fashion to the television screen, exposing the underbelly of the designers' personal life. I liked her, from the Tents at Bryant Park after a PETA—People for the Ethical Treatment of Animals—attack, watched Kelly Klein dodge the same fate with Karl Lagerfeld in hand, and got the security guards to tackle the hecklers when Arnold Scaasi was receiving the CFDA lifetime achievement award at Lincoln Center. I am no purist, but to this day, I avoid fur and am happy to find that the older I get, the less I like red meat. I wear leather shoes, sit on supple skins in my posh Range Rover, I even designed a stunning red sable coat for my sister-in-law Elaine, but as I will describe later on, it was the faux fur fashion show that I had at the Central Park Zoo in the early 1970s that helped set the pattern for my design life.

But back to the Hermans. Those six children spread their seed throughout the area. My aunt Anna, the only daughter and black sheep of the family, was the one I felt closest to. When my mother died, my father, in his panic or wisdom, folded our small family into hers. We moved into a big Victorian house on the only hill in Passaic with unobstructed views of Manhattan from my bedroom window. Those immediate years right after my mother's death were inexplicably the happiest of my young life. I remember my brother Harvey and my cousins Herbie, Nancy, and Phillip playing sexy hide-and-seek up and down the front and back staircase of our very own opera house. *Die Mutter*, Siegfried sings, but at that moment I wasn't listening.

Those few years were the only years that I felt comfort in our family unit. I watched my father put on his riding boots and well-cut dressage jacket, watched him send out feelers to replace his wife, watched him watching me holding the Torah during my Bar Mitzvah, and watched him as he disappeared into the patterns and arms of his new wife and his new life. To this day, people tell me I am a Herman. My brother Harvey insists that I act like a Herman, whatever that means. I do look like my father. My half-brother, Mitchell, stayed within striking distance of his birthplace, surrounded by the Hermans, but he is more his mother's child. As far as I knew, I was the only gay Herman. I remember asking my aunt Anna for the family tree. When I received it, I couldn't find myself until I looked way up in the highest branch, only a twig with no off-shoots.

These days everyone is tracing their DNA. I am 98% Ashkenazi Jew in search of the 2% unaccounted for. There will be no children, no gravestone, my ashes will melt along the shore of the lake I love. Those ashes will mingle with my lover Gene's and my great standard poodle, Mo. But as I see it, I've had a bigger family: a family of friends. So many people that I have wrapped arms with. Although my generation is long gone, there have been others to keep me young. There is still so much to write about. And what about *Die Mutter*, the woman who pampered me, gave me every opportunity to find culture—piano lessons, tap dancing lessons, and drawing lessons. She must have known something about her first child that no one else knew. Her short life was filled with illness that was always present. It meant that there were lots of arguments in the household, mostly about money. And when the end was near, she lashed out at my brother Harvey and myself, accusing us of killing her, of being bad boys, unleashing the frustration and pain she must have felt. In fact, those were the last words we heard from her.

Although, I may look like a Herman, there is much Tannenbaum in the gene pool. When I look at all the pictures of her in my apartment, standing in the uncut Catskill fields, wrapped in an Asian kimono, kabuki-style, shaking a tambourine dressed as a gypsy, on one knee, leaning confidently against my father in the obligatory wedding picture, profiled with three strands of pearls held by an elegant clasp, I can see the sense of style in her choices; the way she avoided and yet conquered the camera was comforting to me. It is a trait I admire to this day.

When I lie in bed in my apartment in New York, I am constantly faced with her lovely attempt to needlepoint. There are stories of her pattern-making facility on our living room floor and her ability to cut on the bias when the fabric was wide enough. My aunt Eleanor gave me a book of Tannenbaum stories. In it, she complains about not being given a chance to go to college and have a chance to play tennis. Why did her brothers receive that privilege? She could make a housedress look chic and her wardrobe was dominated by housedresses that she had made. I've carried no early kitchen tastes with me, no smells that linger, but as I write, she has snuggled up closer to me. There

is no doubt I am my mother's son, even if everything else points to the Herman gene. The last line in Alban Berg's opera, *Wozzeck. Du deine mutter ist tot. Hop hop, hop hop*, has always haunted me because I never really got to know my mother.

The riding boots seemed to work. Within a year, my father had found the woman to take care of his two boys. While my brother and I bonded with my aunt Anna's family, he had made the expected trips to the Catskills to find a mate. She was the polar opposite of my mother—tall, even stately, with an operatic profile; large bosomed, with a distinct Bronx accent. It was a shock to my brother and me and the Tannenbaum family who couldn't believe that he hadn't mourned for even one year. In the very last years of his long life, he told me it was for us that he did it. We needed a mother. Oh, yes, maybe we did, but not that mother.

Right after my mother died, I came down with rheumatic fever diagnosed by the same doctor that had monitored mother during her short life. Like mother, like son. I became the center of attention, and I remember reveling in it. Everyone seemed to rally around me. I even remember being visited by my favorite teacher, Mrs. Peterson, during my recuperation at home.

At this point, the Herman family swooped in. My father's younger, extremely successful brother, Bruno, was childless and, as the story goes, he and his wife, Esther, started to pressure my father for one of his two sons. My brother Harvey thinks it was him. I remember it being me. It was during my recuperative treatment that my uncle Bruno took me to a fancy hotel in Miami. This wounded teenager loved every minute of it. It was a lifestyle that I would eventually enjoy many years later. Poolside, I remember being transfixed by a stunning lifeguard who must have caught that hidden spark of interest and shamelessly displayed his bulging crotch. Nothing happened, but it was one of those early moments that would eventually become the story of my sex life. My uncle and his wife Esther eventually adopted a baby girl, and my brother and I had to deal with an ugly transition, although I have to admit, less so for me than he.

My teen years were clearly dominated by three friends. We became inseparable: Merty, Howie, and Eugene. We did everything together and promised each other that when we went on to college we would all go to the same school. There were girls in our lives, but except for Merty, who found the love of his life in his sophomore year, we talked more about conquests than we experienced our defeats. I know I ducked out of situations that could lead to serious petting and thought I was doing the right thing. Howie quickly became the buffoon who talked the big talk, and Eugene slyly kept close to me, in retrospect feeling very much like me, although he eventually married and became an officer in the Navy with lots of children and a very sullen wife. At one point, he professed his deepest love for me right after I got out of the army and kept his distance from then on.

When I look back at our padded, covered yearbook from 1946, there are pictures and notes under the pictures from my fellow classmates, pages of bobby-socked girls and

PREVIOUS PAGES The Hermans, my father's side of the family, were perfectly poised to face the camera—but note the position of the hands. Six sons and one daughter. Contained and controlled—cool to the touch.

OPPOSITE Big brother and little brother, Harvey, held hands facing the fact that we had to go home after two weeks at sleep-away camp.

ABOVE AND OPPOSITE *Die vater*—my father as horseman. He proudly sat astride his five-gaited horses in Madison Square Garden into his eighties. How many Jewish kids could make that statement?

saddle-shoe'd guys. It all seemed extraordinarily ordinary. A year after the end of World War II, we were grinning into the camera ready to disperse and conquer. At this point in my life, except for my first crush, Jean Bakelar, I'm the only one left. The town of Passaic has morphed into something completely different today, with new immigrants surrounding the comfort of Hassidic Jews living in Passaic Park. I just looked up the population. It is almost, to a person, the same size as it was over 70 years ago. I haven't seen the current high school yearbook, but I doubt if it remotely resembles the one from my time.

When I think of all those early years in Passaic, born into the Great Depression, sheltered by a wide circle of family, seriously bonding with friends during the worst war in history, rocked by a mother's death and a father's awkward transition from middle to upper middle class, with money made during the war's black market, I am amazed at

how easily I seem to have handled the next phase of my life—the years in college, the Army, the acceptance of my life in the gay world. Looking back, it almost seems seamless, like a well-cut sheath, but that's a few chapters away.

DIE MUTTER

Those Saturday mornings selling patterns at my father's silk shop definitely set the pattern for my life in fashion. Those lanky ladies, especially those in the *Vogue Patterns* books became my fantasy friends...but it was my father asking me to hold the pins while he dressed the windows, shuffling on his knees, that I remember most vividly.

He mesmerized me by his balance and his skill, while shoelessly, he arranged waterfalls of prints and plaids for every passerby shopping on a forlorn Monroe Street. Until the very end of his life, he could measure and treasure a yard of fabric like no one else I ever knew, his arm length the perfect yard measurement.

During World War II, fabrics were scarce and he was quite frugal with his selection, often leaving the fabrics to swelter and fade, eventually bundling them and selling them on the sale counter as seconds. My mother's wardrobe was sewn mostly from these end cuts. Once in a while, she would ask for a cut of silk or wool to face an occasion with confidence, but the housedress remained her staple garment. It's easy to see her sense of style in the fading sepia-toned pictures of her short life. Her fabric of choice, sheer rayon Bemberg, which took printing beautifully, with prints that were shy enough to go unnoticed in synagogue.

I've often wondered how my father's later success in life, with money abundant, would have affected her wardrobe. It was my stepmother who filled that gap. Bronx-born, she swept into our lives with a wardrobe influenced by the big city. She filled the tiny house she chose to live in with a squadron of dresses, day to evening, not a housedress in sight. The closet floor was a cadre of pointy-toed shoes, which eventually wreaked havoc on her feet, and created hammer toes that crippled her in later life. She loved pleats and there were many pleated skirts that peaked out from the closet. I am sure my love of pleats began in those closets.

Her blouses and sweaters were neatly folded in tissue paper, And it was in those tissues that I discovered my first sex book. It looked like a librarian's guide to the sex act, its most pornographic word "fellatio"—a word that provoked major bodily pleasure in my teen years.

I don't ever remember fantasizing about wearing her clothes, although I do recall holding a cocktail dress against my body and assuming what I thought was a female slouch.

My fantasy was more sports oriented—to be chosen for the first team in stoop ball seemed more exciting and attainable. My stepmother loved the fact I would be a designer and as my career progressed kept copious files of my success. And I enjoyed designing for her. She was tall, ample breasted, slim hipped, and not afraid to tower over my father's short stature. She always wore those high heels, and, even when they could no longer support her weight, that pointed toe shoe was still her choice.

She actually looked like a middle European opera star until she had a nose job to look more like a Herman. Her ideal was Hedy Lamarr, the great Jewish movie star who had a stellar profile, and she wanted that profile. After the operation, to me, she looked less like a star and stepped back to chorus. Her crown of hair could be magnificent, but she kept the well-coiffed hair in that wig-like perfection too long until the day she died.

My favorite design I made for her was a navy lace gown that she wore to present the five-gaited trophy my father gave in Madison Square Garden every year.

OPPOSITE Passaic had one pretty park and the three of us, mother and sons, are the perfect chorus line, left foot forward, to start the show.

33

OPPOSITE This is my favorite photograph of my mother with all her expectations facing such a short life.

OVERLEAF LEFT
My stylish, favorite uncle Sonny in relaxed splendor, wearing the perfectly balanced double breasted blazer, framing those straight-legged white flannel pants, his life anchored by the slightly scuffed spectator shoes.

OVERLEAF RIGHT
My aunt Marcia and I showing off in the Catskills— a photograph that stops time for me. She was pregnant and I was ready to conquer the world. We loved to dance and remained connected at the swiveled hip until the very end of her life.

There is a stunning picture of her pinning a ribbon on the glorious head of a victorious horse! You can tell she trusted the rider more than the horse.

Two women—my mother Helen who slipped me into a perfectly balanced sweater and shorts, holding my hand as we walked the sparse gardens of Passaic, the woman whose DNA has definitely influenced almost every artistic decision I have ever made, to the stepmother who never saw what was coming when she married a man with two young sons. Both women represent the formative years of my life. *Die Mutter* who still sings to me through all the German lieder I love, and the stepmother who watched a first born devilish child become a clothing designer, not a doctor, not a lawyer, a clothing designer. Now he's writing his memoir, in his 10th decade and becoming the patriarch of his extended family.

These days when I look at the clothing I design for QVC, I often think of my mother, the woman who sewed her own wardrobe to wear around the house—not very far from the designs I create today, call them what you will, they are still housedresses to me.

SCHOOL DAYS

The promise that was made by the four great friends, to go onto school together, didn't work out that way. We actually all applied to the same schools and the only one that the four of us got into was Bradley, a third-ranked university in the town of Peoria, Illinois, something to be said for towns starting with P. I think I was the one who discovered it because, believe it or not, they had courses in fashion design. That's how sheltered I was. New York was beckoning and I found Peoria, but it was not meant to be. Eugene got into Cornell. I found another school with a fashion course, the University of Cincinnati, and Howie and Merty drove ended up in Peoria. That first year in school was the first time I had left home, and I loved it. I never looked back to the easy comfort of my early years. Howie and Merty drove from Cincinnati to Peoria after Thanksgiving break and on the way home were both killed in a car crash, a crash so spectacular it made even the major eastern newspapers. There was a third boy from Passaic who died as well and the whole town mourned, and an important artery of my early life was severed.

Although three of the most significant people in my young life had died, I hadn't yet developed the mourning gene. I was distracted by my new surroundings, and my gregarious nature took over. I loved college, and as indifferent as I had been in high school, that completely changed at the university. Although I was considered an east coaster by my friends, which actually meant a New Yorker, I was really a small town kid from Jersey. Cincinnati was big time, with mini-skyscrapers, seven hills, just like Rome, and a good symphony orchestra. The university was considered a city school

with few out-of-towners and we out-of-towners bonded together. I was even naïve enough to pledge Sigma Chi until they found out that I was Jewish and they told me to get to a synagogue quickly. That synagogue became the Jewish fraternity Sigma Alpha Mu, Sammy for short. Cincinnati had a large German-Jewish population and word got around that I was one of them, which wasn't accurate. Actually, my father's family was part Austrian, especially true with families that had eligible daughters. Boy, was I not eligible.

I stop at this moment to consider me. Here I was a young, not unattractive man, in a strange town pledged to a fraternity of which I eventually became president, a man who made it known that he wanted to be a fashion designer, but also excelled in sports and butch activities. I participated in all the childlike intrigues of dating women without really dating them. The sexiest girls seemed to head toward me, the ones with the raciest reputations. Some of them remained my friends years after I graduated. We did a lot of hot petting with no penetration. I even went up to Hamilton, Ohio, with my buddies to the whorehouses and had sex with some very sweet understanding woman who told me a lot of guys just couldn't get it up and I shouldn't worry—all this happening while my friends were moaning with great pleasure in the next room. I'm sure there were people who might have questioned my sexuality or considered me effeminate, but they never said it to my face.

To this day, it is my energy that people seem to remember. I went through college with top honors. I was considered the most talented student in my class. And I was responsible for moving my fraternity from the Jewish ghetto onto campus, neighboring the very blonde Gentile girls of Tri Delta on Clifton Avenue.

There was never any thought of my staying in Cincinnati. I realized that New York was where I really belonged. My parents drove the turnpikes to attend my graduation and we drove back to the east coast together, which would become my home for the rest of my life. Again, it all seemed so easy.

With all of my newfound friends, there was no one who anchored me to the Midwest. There were two who were also in the fraternity house that remained in my life until their deaths. My roommate, Hoppy, who became a much-admired architect, was responsible for building the model city of Columbia, near Baltimore. And Dr. Bill Serbin, the most operatic character I ever knew, who married, had four children, and admitted his homosexuality in his mid-sixties. There were others that held onto the strings of friendship. The woman who was my muse, Dossie, the beautiful misfit of Tri Delta who ended her life tending a water garden filled with frogs, none of whom turned into a prince. There was also the woman who became one of Cincinnati's wealthiest benefactors and the one who pushed me far enough sexually to scare the shit out of me. She wanted a serious relationship and I was waiting for a sign to accept that relationship. Obviously, it never came to be and years later she teased me mercilessly for what I missed while completely accepting my chosen lifestyle with Gene.

OPPOSITE Dossie, my first muse, was a competitive student at the University of Cincinnati—her sense of irreverence for the rulemakers helped set me onto my very long fashion journey.

OPPOSITE

Showing off on the beaches of Cannes—army-buffed and ready to conquer my newfound secret sex life.

The University of Cincinnati has remained a constant in my life. Fifteen years ago they gave me an honorary doctorate. My father was very proud to call me Dr. Herman. I have taught many classes over the years at their very successful school of design. I've even hired a few assistants from the school. It is certainly a much finer school now than over half a century ago. I think it's easygoing nature, far from the hot center of fashion, allowed me to cultivate a personality to compete with the competitiveness of fashion without collapsing under pressure. I liked everyone, for the most part. I still do today. As I write this, it's over 70 years ago that I graduated.

After graduation, I quickly got my first job as coffee boy for a very commercial dress house in Philadelphia called L'Aiglon. I was hired because the head designer saw me as a sexual object and that object stayed out of reach until I was drafted into the army. I vividly remember a note left on my desk by the house models. "We love you. You are adorable, but we think you should use deodorant." I didn't even know deodorants were available in my sheltered Midwestern and Passaic life. I have more than made up for it. To this day, I am known by how great my perfume smell is, vetiver in any form. The silhouette of New York was getting closer. The sidestep to Philadelphia kept me intriguingly close, but it was another two years as an Army corporal that opened me up to both my true sexuality and my need to start competing in the big town. *New York, New York, that wonderful town*, one of my auditioning songs in my brief show biz career, but we will talk about that later.

THE ARMY

Not many people I talk to much remember the Korean War, less than five years after the war-to-end-all-wars, ended. All able-bodied young men were subject to the draft. Just out of college and being very able-bodied, I was drafted. My father was elated. His son didn't have a heart condition, but I'll never know what he really felt. It might have made a man out of his son, the designer. I never asked him, but he seemed proud that his son was serving his country. I was his offering. Truth told, I almost felt relieved. Korea seemed far off and put Philadelphia out of my life. I was a good soldier, shockingly good. Once again, I seemed to inspire friendships, probably due to my flirtatious nature and the need for male companionship.

I spent my basic training at Fort Dix, New Jersey, a few hours and a dusty world apart from Passaic. In retrospect, the close proximity was a good way to adjust. The army had just integrated. Oh, yes, in 1950, there were still black barracks. I will never forget the first time I called cadence for a platoon of the most brilliantly coordinated new black recruits. They towered over me and stepped out way beyond my short legs. It was the last week they were segregated. Once integrated, the pace became easier to handle.

Anyone who has ever been in the army will understand how demanding basic training can be. I didn't fall in love with my rifle, but I watched many of my buddies massaging their M1s, putting them lovingly to bed at night, waking up with them in the morning. I never was a crack shot. I blame that on my inability to close my left eye and not adjusting to the sight line. There were lots of bruised noses. It took weeks to get a uniform that fit my small frame. I looked like the classic sad sack private who stepped into the wrong picture frame, but I flourished. I made friends. No sex. Not yet.

The first shock came when my platoon sergeant wanted me to share his private quarters. At first, I thought it was because I was a good soldier, but within two nights he had his prick out and tried to force me into bed. I can't believe I got out, but not before he had awakened that part of me that was just waiting to be taken to the Promised Land. There was also a soldier in the next barracks that zeroed in on my radar. He was possibly the most beautiful man I'd ever seen and I found myself searching him out. Within a month, we had become best buddies. He has stayed in my fantasy life for over 70 years. First as a buddy, then as a rejected lover, then, as the years went by, a successful movie director, married with five children. We actually never reconnected, but in my head, I always wanted to apologize for rejecting his advances. He was the very first man who wanted to make love to me.

My complete barracks went to Korea and I personally knew of three men who never came home. I cunningly made friends with the man who ran the placement operation at Fort Dix and got him to keep me there training the new recruits until he was able to ship me off to Europe—to Germany and the alpine peaks of Bavaria. If life has moments that set the patterns of your life, this was that moment for me. Shipped as a lone soldier with no platoon connections, I found a buddy who within two days at sea was reading Heinrich Heine to me and trying to figure out how we could stay connected when we reached Europe. We didn't remain connected, but listening to the European radio stations as we anchored offshore, waiting to disembark, I could hear the whisper of languages so foreign and yet so comforting to me. We landed in Bremerhaven and traveled all night to southern Germany. Little lights on little houses leading the way and we arrived at the town of Sonthofen, the repo depot for all troops landing in Europe. All this happened at night. So, when I woke up the next morning, in a Kaserne that had been built for Hitler's youth, I found myself attached to a motley group of privates without a definite destination, all of us silhouetted against the most beautiful snowcapped peaks I had ever seen.

I still wasn't sure where I would be stationed, but as far as I was concerned this was where I wanted to stay. My memory is a little fuzzy, but somehow, I found out that they were looking for a mapmaker and within a day I had ripped apart some brown paper bags, Scotch-taped them into a canvas shape and drew maps, all kinds of maps. The colonel, who had a cushy job at the Kaserne, asked me if I could learn to lecture

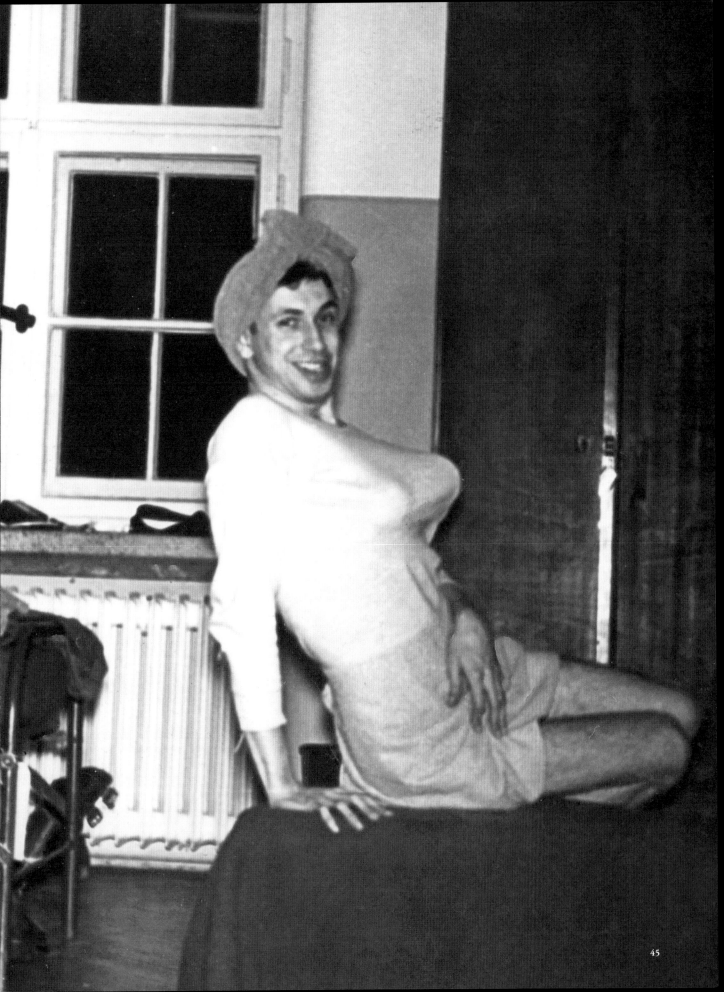

the troops in Germany on army protocol and take over the art studio that was applying signage for the barracks. So, for the next year, I became star greeter for all the troops entering Germany.

Up until 30 years ago, I would still hear from many of the men that came through that depot. I was the front man while the major could fuck to his heart's content in his private hideaway up the mountain. The art studio personnel were almost all German and I was prepared to hate them but I didn't. I'm sure most had been in the Nazi party, but somehow, they tiptoed around the dirt and wooed me with their Bayerische accents and schinkenbrot. I believe the beauty of the countryside, especially the snowcapped mountains and the gregarious group of army buddies, kept a smile on my face. How lucky I was to have found show biz in the barracks.

I was in khaki heaven. The new world of this drafted corporal from Passaic, New Jersey, suddenly surrounded by history and art on a picture postcard continent, so many men comfortably running around in the underground shadows of their sexuality. Suddenly the postcard wasn't a picture. It was the reality and became the building block for my life as an open homosexual. I didn't run off swooning into the sunset, but I began to understand that the sun would set and my life would be a part of it. It's amazing how many times a room full of straight guys, well, almost straight guys, would play the female role while imitating the sexual dance between the sexes. In my case, I flexed my masculine muscles. Never once did I remember playing la femme.

I can actually pinpoint the time when I realized that Europe would always be in my future. It happened soon after the repo depot left those sheltering mountains and moved to the grittier side of Germany—a small industrial town, Zweibrucken. What it lacked in beauty it made up for in its proximity to the European countryside—trips to Paris, the Rivera, Capri, and Venice on a weekend pass. At this point, I was sent for a refresher course on proper propaganda, which was being taught at the Dachau concentration camp. Two weeks that peeled away the veneer that I had cultivated when I first arrived in Germany. The reality of those footprints on the ceiling hit hard. My relationship to the German mentality abruptly challenged by this brutal reminder of World War II.

When I got back to Zweibrucken, I went to pick up my mail and from behind the mailman's screen a voice of many octaves asked me, "Where have you been all my life?" His name was, quite appropriately, Dick, and was he a beauty, just butch enough to protect his flaming gestures, but gay enough to frighten me. I initially avoided him, but not for long. He began to peel away the all-male underbelly of army living. I think he had almost every lieutenant in the Kaserne. As he put it, we became sisters, a new relationship to me.

Our most important trip together was the one to Venice. Dick had contacted a wealthy expatriate who lived in a palace on the Grand Canal and we were to meet him with a friend at the Piazza San Marco, but only after we had walked the square in order for

OPPOSITE I may not be around when we have our first gay president, but I told Pete Buttigieg, "Bubbelah, I've waited 90 years for it to happen, and you better not disappoint me."

them to judge our butch credentials. We passed muster and thus began a weekend of such lust my knees still buckle when I think about it: parties overlooking the Grand Canal, gondolas to the Lido to fuck in the sand, food that spoiled me for the rest of my life, like a simple green pea floating in a pool of fine angel hair spaghetti and, most importantly, the first suitor for my affection, not my penis.

His name was Arthur Jeffries, and he had the most beautiful gondola in all of Venice. Before I realized what was happening, he had me visiting him in London and back to Venice, slipping out of my uniform and into the civilian world he was trying to get me to join once I was discharged. He was a part of the heady world-weary group circling around the doyenne of Venice, Peggy Guggenheim. One of Arthur's close friends was Philip Johnson, the famous architect, and we became a foursome with Philip's younger lover, John Hohnsbeen. All this happened the last few months of my tour of duty, simultaneously with my complete acceptance of my sexuality. And, oh, how easy it was.

Now, almost 70 years later, while writing this memoir, I googled Arthur and was shocked to find that a book about his life had just been published in England, *Arthur Jeffries: A Life in Art.* He apparently was a mighty force in the gay world of Europe, entertaining royalty and perfecting the art of drag while doing it. He was outed by his gondoliers after he fired them for not getting the Duke and Duchess of Windsor back to their hotel. His sin was his sexual orientation and Venice banned him for that. Just nine years after our romance, he committed suicide in Paris, leaving a large estate and a reputation interesting enough to fill a book years later. The big shock to me was that, in retrospect, he was my father's age and there was an uncanny resemblance between the two, *Mein Vater,* Parsifal, Siegmund sings.

Suddenly, the inevitable happened. My tour was over. I would be going home, leaving this operatic existence on a continent I felt should be my home. I tried to apply to get into design school in Paris, but the mechanism for soldiers staying in Europe hadn't been set up yet. I even thought of reenlisting to stay, but that thought went nowhere quickly. It still amazes me how easily I fell into the cadence of the army world. Was it those mountains, the history of Europe, the buffed backsides I marched with? Was it my ability to move easily between the gay and straight world?

Reality stepped in and I sailed back to America. Seven days riding the 30-foot high waves that kept us off the decks and close to the garbage cans of puke so different than that silent night when I heard the rustle of Europe as we approached Bremerhaven. I had made many friends in the Army, as is my way. I kept in touch with many of them. Little by little, most faded away. A few, Hardy, Dick, and Bob, remain alive in my memory, but they too have all gone now, but Europe has not faded away. It still sharply defines my life. I know it affected my design career, my love for classical music, my food choices, and my taste in art, especially Austrian.

Folded away in my wallet are my army credentials. They have yellowed with age. I've

never taken advantage of my veteran status, never used a veterans hospital, or marched in a Veterans Day parade. The youngest generation of my extended family find it unusual for their gay uncle to have been a soldier. But it was at a time when being gay meant being silent, and that silence produced its own rules of the game.

It was all underground—in many ways more intoxicating, forbidden fruit, if you were not caught. We've come a long way today, and for someone my age it still can be shocking to see same-sex affection casually displayed publicly, but how sweet it is to see it.

To have an openly gay man running for president, and a nephew transitioning to becoming my niece in full view. In a world filled with turmoil, it gives me hope. I only wish Gene could have been here to see it happening.

HOME AGAIN

I spent two years in khaki from private to corporal, the last year swooning into the European lifestyle. It was back to New York to work and become a clothing designer. I moved into a rooming house just off of Fifth Avenue and Central Park, one of those leftover mansions that collapsed into the fetal position and catered to the young New York wannabes, nothing but a room, a hall phone, and a shared bathroom. I loved it. It was my own, no one to share my idle hours with, and a landlady who was a breast cancer survivor. She had a mastectomy in the late 1940s and would quickly show you the scars to prove it.

My previous connection before I was drafted to the hat designer, Fred Frederics, proved to be most valuable. He was immediately on the case of getting me a job and before I knew what was happening, I had become the dessert course for his weekend orgies. All this taking place in his Park Avenue apartment with his buddies, probably the most famous being Jerry Zipkin. It was at one of those evenings, while waiting for the participants who were arriving from California, that I met the gentleman who I would give my life to for 40 years, but I am getting ahead of myself.

The first job I got was with one of Fred's society friends, the Countess Illinska, known as Fira Benenson in the fashion world. She was a designer who catered to the wealthy working class ladies of Park Avenue, a designer who sold her soul to brocades and taffetas. Although she did sell to high-end stores, most of her business was semi-custom for her customers—ladies who had time to lunch, but preferred to volunteer at museums, hospitals, and soup kitchens. Actually, I was a glorified delivery boy, as was the gentleman whose job I took. His name was John Moore. He went on to have a high profile, but a brief career, and might be most famous today as Norman Norell's lover. I liked Fira, but my problem was that she always kept her hand over her mouth and

OPPOSITE This Playbill is all I have left of my Broadway debut in *La Plume de Ma Tante*. I swung those ropes for six months, proud of my athletic talents. I wasn't quite ready for stardom, but it was good enough to appreciate the applause.

nose when she talked. I think she had a nose job that she was unhappy with. That and her alto overtones made for difficult conversations. When she asked me to drape a sleeve or heat the coffee, it all sounded the same.

The best part of the job was that at the end of the day. I would dash down 57th Street—our offices were between Fifth and Sixth avenues, to her home at 333 East 57th, between First Avenue and Sutton Place, to make sure her vodka was chilled and spiked with lemon. It was served in the most beautiful cut-glass pitcher, and once in a while she would offer me a sip. But mostly, she was busy keeping her white Russian compatriots entertained, always magnanimous with her booze. Fred kept sending me to other friends, even the great Pauline Trigère, who never bought a sketch in her life. For weeks, I sketched what I thought she would love and dropped them off never to see them again. Years later, she got a good laugh when I told her that I was sure she would have loved my sketches if she had only seen them.

This, to the woman who had the most skilled scissors that she used instead of a sketch pen. I think I got the job with Oleg Cassini on my own. He must have stood me up 20 times before he gave in and hired me to work from his home in the East Sixties. All of this was what I called biting off the edges, something I perfected in my long career. Uptown designers were one thing, but Seventh Avenue is where I wanted to be. And my next job was for one of Seventh Avenue's more tony labels, Herbert Sondheim, who was the father of Stephen Sondheim, and a man of manners and white glove reputation. His chief designer was Andrew Woods, a gentleman who had arrived a decade before from Indiana with his best friend, Bill Blass. This was the first time I felt a part of the Seventh Avenue campus, 530 Seventh Avenue, on the top floors, with a setback makeshift terrace to sun yourself during lunchtime. Andrew was a good teacher and became a close friend. We watched the seesaw of our careers over the years. Mine, eventually riding high; his, bellied up to the bottle, preferably gin, ending up in a lonely burial plot in an ex-pat zone north of Barcelona.

In retrospect, my DNA as a designer was first nurtured at my next job for Martini Design. Sylvan Rich, who was my next boss and a close friend, owned one of Seventh Avenue's most successful cocktail dress houses.

Dresses still dominated the Garment Center. Sportswear, and the designers dancing around the center, remained hidden on the side streets.

I became Sylvan's shadow assistant for almost four years, eventually achieving the status of design assistant and jack of all trades, from stock boy to formidable competitor to his stable of designers.

My next move was a big upgrade. I would actually be the designer, not just the sketcher, for a company named Wrappi. I believe it was named after someone's aunt with talent. She was one of the many unsung dressmaker designers, turning out America's fashion mediocrity. But she was good, good enough to have her name on the label. Her business was a part of a conglomerate owned by the Kalish family. Their star designer was

Anne Fogarty. I believe she was the first female designer to build a licensing business bigger than her core business. Even though I was the third designer in the company, I had my own room and my own sample hands, and boy did my competitive spirit kick in. We would show our week's work every Friday afternoon to the bosses, including Miss Wrappi. This was the year that Yves Saint Laurent conquered the world and, like everyone else, I was influenced by his A-line and chemise dressing. It took me all week, and I almost lost my assistant, while draping and re-draping my little black chemise. It ended with a white ruffle at the neckline and Wrappi must have seen it, snooping around my room after hours. Just as I sent it out with my favorite model, I heard Wrappi say, "I suppose the next dress will be for a clown." I was fired that evening and walked away from Seventh Avenue to try my luck in show biz.

Walking away was easy. I was already in a full-blown relationship with Gene, and between his steady teacher's paycheck and my unemployment, we made it work. We were living in the heart of the Village, had two dogs, a fifth-floor walk-up with a fire escape and a little hot waterless shack in the Hamptons. Yes, in the Hamptons. For me, it was a dream come true. I was going to be in show business. What chutzpa for a guy who hadn't studied singing or dance, and who had flunked out of Herbert Berghof's acting classes. And, of course, there was living in the Greenwich Village of the 1950s, where the sun was brighter, the trees greener, the streets more complex in their grid, and filled with people who were beginning to stretch their creative muscle right after the two wars. Anything seemed possible. I was in love with the city and the man who shaped my life forever. And I was lucky.

My very close friend, the designer Arnold Scaasi, who had defied all odds and became famous in his early twenties, decided to sponsor my new career. Arnold was one of the few designers to hang the couture designation on his label. His over-the-top creations have graced some of our country's most famous First Ladies.

Arnold never thought I was a good designer and told me that constantly. We signed a contract that his lawyer drew up and between unemployment and his generous gesture, I started singing lessons, dancing lessons, and auditioning. There were many afternoons that I sat on the stoop across from our apartment on West 4th Street with our two dogs, Senta and Liffy, sunning myself as I cruised the delivery boys going by. West 4th Street was a perfect microcosm of the Village, with a generous greengrocer, Brignole's, and the Florence Meat Market, which is still there to this very day, down the block from the famous Stonewall Bar and Washington Square Park, just two express stops from the Garment Center, but there's no longer a clothes rack in sight.

I went to open cattle calls and seldom got past two bars of music before I got the hook. At one of those calls, I arrived with my sheet music, a patter song with a range of four notes called "Breathless." This audition was for a show called, *Girl Crazy*. Almost everyone I saw had arrived with their own accompanist. Those that didn't have one used the house pianist and this particular house pianist was "the" John Kander. I didn't make it even halfway through the song before a voice in the dark said, "Thank you." Many years later, I told John this story and, whether he was lying or not, he said he remembered me. He is a good man and a great composer.

My active career in the theater consisted of two summer stock performances, one in Beverly, Massachusetts, and the other in Indianapolis, Indiana. Both were as Evil Eye Fleagle in *L'il Abner*. I think I got the part because they had a costume that fit only short people. The other was a stunner, a feature player in a very successful Broadway musical, *La Plume de Ma Tante*. I got this part because I was a pretty good gymnast and the most famous scene in the show opened the second act, four monks waking up to ring the church bells, all choreographed to a set of ropes that eventually had you flying out over the orchestra, and God forbid you let go.

Once I got over a combination of stage fright and the constant bullying by the star of the show, Robert Clary, who just died this year, thought I looked too much like him, and who had learned the techniques of torture as a prisoner in Auschwitz, I loved my new gypsy existence. I was good enough so that the David Merrick Organization, who were the producers of the show, asked me to go on the road with a show called, *Carnival*, starring Anna Maria Alberghetti, in a featured role, no less. There was no chance I would have accepted this road show when I was so in love with Gene and would not leave him. I also started to take singing seriously and had promised my new teacher I wouldn't sing professionally until he had reconstructed the voice. Who knew I would soon sound like Pavarotti, and eventually have the same accompanist, Gildo DiNunzio, work with me in the opera world?

I sang two leading roles at the Amato Opera House on the Bowery. The fatuous tenor in *Die Fledermaus*, and almost all of Rodolfo in *La Bohème*. I know it sounds pompous to say, but I had a beautiful natural sound to my voice, yet I was a terrible musician. I couldn't read music easily and, although my pronunciation of French, Italian, and German was good, I never really took the time to know what I was saying. I was too starstruck by my high notes and my singing teacher, Tony Frisell, that I never finished polishing my technique or maybe it was me who was never able to do that. Those of you who have any knowledge of how difficult it is to sing operatically will sympathize. I continued taking singing lessons for the next 15 years, twice a week in the theater district. It became my therapy and my calling card to my love of opera and classical music.

During this period, I also made pirated recordings of famous American singers. I could easily imitate Elvis Presley, Andy Williams, and both of the Everly Brothers. My recording name was Chet Avery and everything was done in the middle of the night in the Brill Building. A skeleton crew would overdub 10 times to fill out the orchestra and I would sing in any key they would ask me to. Somewhere in my apartment, I have those recordings. They were all made for European consumption and, boy, was I big in Holland.

While I was in *La Plume*, most of my days were free and a friend asked me to design a line of clothing for his new business—his funding secure, and a showroom a few blocks south of the theater—I jumped at the chance. Just me, no other designers to compete with, a clean slate. The only stipulation was that the sizing would be called Junior. In fact, the name of the company would be Junior Forum. This was a new exciting market on the avenue and some of the most talented designers were championing that fit: Liz Claiborne for Youth Guild, Betty Carol, Mr. Mort, and Anne Klein for Junior Sophisticates. If there is any equivalent to this new junior market today, it would be the activewear world. Up until the 1960s, everyone wanted to look like their mother. The junior market flipped the script and the designers I mentioned pioneered that movement. Suddenly, there seemed to be purpose to my design. No more taffeta flowers, satin bows, and side draping. It was a complete collection, day into evening, which was its strength, but from a production standpoint, its weakness. Too many fabrics, too many patterns, but *Women's Wear Daily* came to see it and said, "A star [was] born." It was not the *Women's Wear* we know of today. It was more the industry's newspaper. Not many bitchy belches from those pages at that time, straight reporting with no agenda that I knew of. So here I was, a star on the side streets of Seventh Avenue and a gypsy performer on Broadway, with paychecks that made me blink with surprise. The next few months were glorious. I loved the people at Junior Forum and life on the stage became easier. I would just swing out a little higher at every performance and kept working on the break in my newfound operatic voice.

My love affair with Gene was ever ripe. I had never met anyone like him. He gave purpose to face those tricky times. He began to peel away the protective layers of rigidity in my Virgo personality. He was my opposite, a Pisces. And, yes, opposites do attract. There was no small talk in his repertoire and suddenly my tiptoe experiments with books and music became a reality. His scholarly friends, mostly teachers, seduced me into listening, and I know many of them did not understand the attraction he had for me. "Good, God. What does anyone do with a clothing designer?" They said it would never last. I tend to write romantically when I talk about Gene and our lives together, so bear with me. We had our difficult moments, but like everything else in our relationship, we had great respect for each other.

La Plume put up its closing notice and I had already turned down going on the road, but my newfound fame on Seventh Avenue kept me busy. There was no way I would leave this young, exciting company. I was already deeply into the next collection and trying to figure out why everyone seemed to like my first collection. Oh, we designers are an insecure lot. That is probably our strength. Lots of negative energy whipped into a positive facade. Then it all fell apart. I arrived at work one morning and there were padlocks on the doors. Our backers turned out to be part of the Jewish mafia and there was hanky panky with the Teamsters Union. Shelley, our president, and all the workers suddenly disappeared. I was once again out of work.

At that very moment, I suddenly realized I was thinking of my life as two. I would need to start making decisions that would enhance our lives together. Gene had the ability to face the future head on. I could sidestep. Remember, I was tap dancing when I was five.

Together, we made the decision to move from our Romeo and Juliet walkup on Fourth Street to a semi-classy new apartment on West 12th Street. It was just a few blocks north, but worlds apart. Gene loved it. He could see the ships gliding down the Hudson River to their exotic destinations. The year was 1960 and, as if on target, I got a call from the gentleman who owned the very hot label, Mr. Mort. They had been watching this young designer and would I become a part of their stable? Oh, yes, I would. And I did. I never looked back to show biz.

Both Gene and I were into our early thirties and a sense of stability had set in. He was teaching English to overachieving students in Chappaqua, New York, a glittery Westchester town comfortably north of the city. We already had a car and a summer shack in Southampton, three dogs, and a very active love life.

He was just beginning his first book, which became, *Home is Where You Start From*, and his family had already wrapped us into their lives—my family still tip- toeing on the edge of acceptance.

SKETCHING

How did it all start? How did I learn to control the flow of ink to paper and draw the shadow lines of a pencil sketch? It always seemed like a natural gesture, a gesture that probably started when we were taught the technique of penmanship in the second grade. We were part of a test studio to print rather than use cursive lettering. Our script had to emulate the typewriter. It all looked too boring, so I began to add "flourishes" to my letters—letters and sketches that are the essence of this memoir. Even the artists I admire have touched their canvases with a sketching style: Raoul Dufy, Henri Matisse, and Georges Rouault, with his juicy black lines that dominate his canvases.

I am a good sketcher, my right hand can sweep confidently over a blank piece of paper, pen in hand, and create an instant world of linear wonder. I have chronicled every trip with Gene in little four-by-six sketch books.

Hundreds of sketches, most of them drawn in our hotel room, looking through the window at the ancient profile of Europe. Bathrooms seem to dominate the portfolio, closely followed by wallpapered sitting rooms, and unmade beds.

City to city, Milan to Venice by way of Capri. The Alto Adige and the burnished peaks of the Dolomites. The high Alps of Austria and Germany, shadowing the town where I was stationed during my Army days. London, Paris, Barcelona, Stockholm,

VILLA SERBELLONI
FROM THE TERRACE

59

OPPOSITE The dress
on the model Cheryl
Tiegs exemplifies the
Mr. Mort look. And,
if I may say so, it still
looks modern today.

**OVERLEAF LEFT
AND RIGHT** The one
woman whose beauty
inspired my designs
is the legendary Ali
McGraw. She wore
my little pleated dress
in the movie *Love
Story* and I've been
married to her ever
since. These looks,
from the now-defunct
McCall's magazine,
are perfect examples
of my decade in
the hot center.

Vienna, Salzburg—quick, secure black lines from my Pilot pen. No sketch taking longer than boiling an egg.

So many quick takes of Gene in repose, writing in his diary, luxuriating in a bathtub after a day of sightseeing.

Restaurants filled with privileged diners, hotel bars overstocked with single malt scotch, olive pits, and empty barstools.

Plane trips to Hawaii, Alaska, Brazil; quick takes of palm trees, glaciers, and my favorite subject, mountains. So many tables laden with crystal and white linen napkins. Windows looking outward to infinity.

My favorite moments in Bryant Park and the perpendicular thrust of Midtown.

Two rumpled tennis shirts hanging to dry after a scruffy match on the unattended tennis courts of the Villa Serbelloni.

Fashion sketches by the thousands, from the stick-like attempts during my Bar Mitzvah to the round, pretentious ladies who represented my college years.

Those days, I used a light lead pencil and colored markers before the final flourish of my pen.

If anything, seven decades later, there is more of a sense of security that comes with age. I've tried my hand at painting, even built a studio to paint in, and the few canvases I've finished are painted in quick strokes, diluting oil to watercolor consistency.

All of these sketches are the camera of my life, long before the Smart Phone photograph existed. Most of them have been lying lifeless, those four-by-six sketch books, sharing space with all of my aging publicity pictures, some of which are well-framed on the staircase walls of my duplex in Manhattan.

Writing this memoir has given them new meaning—quick sketches that fill the memory bank of that life.

MR. MORT

The next ten years became my decade. Tapped by the owners of Mr. Mort, a paycheck every two weeks, a bank account, a credit line, and Gene teaching closer to the city in the affluent town of Chappaqua, surrounding us with teachers that were fast becoming close friends. We had our tiny, hot-waterless shack on the east end of Long Island and I was encouraging Gene to write during the summers when he wasn't teaching. It was a different time. I was already in my late thirties, looking like an aging teenager. Gene, full featured, looking like a radical writer from some middle European country or, Jesus Christ. The world on Seventh Avenue was waking up from its mom and pop wartime slumber. I had already apprenticed for 10 years, moved from job to job, from Martini Design to Junior Forum. My expectations of my own

PREVIOUS PAGES
Here is my quick
sketch of the iconic
label for Mr. Mort.

OPPOSITE If anything
represents the Mr.
Mort look it is these
"Kitty Foyle" box
pleated dresses.
I had a thing about
prissy meets fashion.
To this day, I remain
consistent in my love
of pleats and purity.

**OVERLEAF LEFT AND
RIGHT** If clothing
represents time, then
these two photos are
good examples.
Women's Wear Daily
caught me smoking,
left, and my PR
people put me on
a pedestal, *right*.
Thankfully, I gave
up smoking. It's
harder for me
these days to climb
up onto a pedestal.

label had to be earned. Arnold Scaasi, was one of the few who jumped out of the gate early and stayed there.

I loved Seventh Avenue, five buildings on the west side of the street with a few side street stragglers; a wide avenue that caught the sunlight straight from 10 am to 2 pm, perfect timing for all the tailors to sun themselves during their yenta lunch breaks. There were the sounds of the swirling, stirring spoons in the tipped glasses of the egg cream vendors. The chauffeured owners of 550 and 530 came to work long after the sample hands, lunch in hand, began using the freight elevators. I ate lunch almost every day downstairs at 498 Seventh Avenue in a very Spartan restaurant called Wilkerson's, sharing space with my fellow designers, waiting and watching an imaginary chess game, moving from pawn to one of the castles, looking to catch the Queen.

Mr. Mort was part of a large operation, three or four divisions owned by the Cole family. They were the first company to feature a French designer, Jules-François Crahay for Nina Ricci. I became the second designer in the Mr. Mort division. The designer who started the company was a woman named Lee Evans. It was her sense of style that set the tone for the label and she was good, very good.

The man who started the label, Mort Goldman, hence the name, lost it quickly to the Cole family and spent the rest of his life trying to find the magic again. Lee was long gone and there were already cracks in the business, which, as historians would remember, had a very elegant butler bending over in a state of subservience on the label. If anyone finds one in their search through vintage racks, swipe it for me. For five years, I worked my ass off, quickly becoming the Number One designer for the company, with too many sample hands to feed. One of my closest friends became the best technical assistant of my life. She came to me one day and said it's difficult to work with a close friend and remain friends so let's call it quits. She went on to become the chief assistant for Donna Karan and Louis Dell'Olio at Anne Klein.

We had factories everywhere. One, on the Palisades, could have produced cars, it was so big. Mr. Cole, the gentleman, and his much-beleaguered son, Richard, had completely lost touch with reality. Production men were stealing. The products suffered and the bloom quickly faded. Not for me: I was still considered someone to watch, and when the business eventually closed, I was still considered desirable. There was a sudden scramble to acquire the label Mr. Mort by all those who worked there: The sales staff, the production men, the Cole family led by Arthur's daughter Sheila, who became a very close friend of mine. Everyone wanted it but me. I wanted my own label. I wanted to be my own Mr. I couldn't seem to extricate myself from the label. I did get one man from Dallas interested in my name, but it meant spending too much time away from New York, so I started a freelance studio to make my living.

My first job as a freelancer was for the giant Russ Togs Corporation. I convinced them to try to go upscale with a sportswear collection that would be sold at stores like Lord & Taylor, my personal favorite. They gave me a small showroom which, much

Nickel is what we call the prettiest and palest of the great new grays, a gray that is almost as soft as spring itself.
You see it in the pleated dresses below, all gentle movement; in the fresh dirndl-skirted suits coming up, some
with long, soft-sleeved white crepe shirts. One way you'll see it is with shades of copper—light to bright copper patent, pigskin,
calf; dark, copper-tinted legs; tawny, coppered lipstick. The other way you'll see it: with the shine of white—
on the next pages. The shades of copper, opposite, going clockwise from the top: Sheer, dark coppery stockings by Hanes,

WITH NICKEL: SHADES OF COPPER

$1.65. Square-toed, thick-heeled
shoes with brown patent trim
by Charles Jourdan, $34.
Luggage-locked pigskin briefcase bag by Ruza Creations, $15.
Double-buckled pigskin belt by Elegant, $8. Pigskin
envelope by Ruza Creations, $10. Patent leather bag by Gia, $18.
Pigskin roll bag by Bagatelle, $36. The warm, soft
coppered lips are slicked with Max Factor's new
"CopperCotta" UltraLucent Creme Iridescent Lipstick.

This page, left:
Pleated crepe
dress with white
collar and cuffs
by Stan Herman
for Mr. Mort,
$55. Flower-
textured nickel
pantie stockings
by Berkshire.
Right: Pleated
dress with a
white rose by
Westbury Fashions,
of textured rayon,
$30. Nickel
and white checked
sheer stockings
by Roman Stripe.
Both hats by Adolfo.
See Shopping Guide
Beauty details,
page 220.
Accessory shopping
details for opposite
page, page 214.

ANTONIO

TAD YAMASHIRO

against their wishes, I painted white. White showrooms were not yet popular. Catholic ivory held sway. People felt it was easier on the eyes and the clothes. All I wanted on those white walls was a painting of the fields in Watermill by my good friend Jane Freilicher. I had bought it at the Tibor De Nagy Gallery, charging it to Russ Togs, and found three simple pods of rattan tables and chairs. When the president, Eli Russo, found out that I had spent $1,500 for the painting, he sent it back to the gallery and no matter how hard I tried, they wouldn't sell it back to me. Many years later, that exact painting sold in the high six-figure category. The only other original Freilicher, except for a lovely pastel I have, is the canvas she gave me when I told her I didn't know how to stretch my own. In the living room of my home in the country is a Stan Herman painting of my first hot-waterless shack comfortably sitting on her gracious gift.

After much shuffling, the name Mr. Mort was bought for a measly $15,000 by our head salesman, Glenn Thompkins. Mr. Cole couldn't or didn't want to top his bid. The last thing I wanted to do was to go back in business with Glenn and his pretentiousness. which included a Rolls-Royce that he used as a pimpmobile, cruising the avenue after hours. The gentleman who was the brains of Russ Togs was Henry Benach, not a part of the company's close-knit Sephardic Jewish family. During one of my many conversations with him, he asked me why I didn't want to go into business with my ex-partners. I told him I thought it was fraught with failure, that we needed good management and lots of money to get it back into competitive shape. And in a quick aside, that I *would* do it if Russ Togs bought the name back from them. That aside was the kernel that grew quickly. Within months, he wrangled the name from Glenn and hired him to run the showroom. He also hired a good man named Jerry Paterson as the CEO, and although I didn't have my own label, they made me president and I kissed ass to have them give me equal billing—Stan Herman for Mr. Mort.

Those next five years were glorious. Every designer should have that touched-by-an-angel moment. It seemed I could do nothing wrong. It was an intoxicating time. The destructive hyper-1960s was my decade. I began to wear bells around my neck so my partners could hear me coming. I said it was to protest the Vietnam War, but I lied. I had the most dedicated sample room—eight women of diverse backgrounds who worked their magic. One of the largest companies proudly backed us. Assistants like Barbara Larson and Jan Johnson kept me focused while becoming my muses. I was good copy for the press, one of the new vocal young designers now secretly pushing 40 that was shaking up the open-to-buys in department stores. The Seventh Avenue campus, as I called it, accepted this newly revitalized company with welcoming arms. It took me close to 15 years to break through, which would be an eternity in today's world. I was never given a tutorial on branding a company. The global aspect of competition was still decades away. American designers were just beginning to decide on their own hemlines, looking at licensing their names, strutting down runways.

OPPOSITE Once again, Antonio Lopez captured the mood of Mr. Mort for *Glamour* magazine. I still love the touch of lace and velvet making love in a silhouette that remains modern to this day.

LEFT Is he, or isn't he? Kenn Duncan snapped this picture for *After Dark* magazine. The beauteous Naty Abascal with the shameless Stan Herman became my favorite picture.

OVERLEAF LEFT AND RIGHT Back in the 1960s, this *trompe-l'œil* dress set Seventh Avenue on its ears. I had a group of ladies hand-knit them in the Bronx and produce them in far-off China. There were seven styles and this was one of the most popular. The vintage sample you see was found by Todd Oldham in a thrift shop and given back to me by Fern Mallis. If anyone still has one, treat it well—it's my good luck charm.

The word sportswear was just a whisper. It was still called the dress business in America. Paris was the grand wizard; Milan the ultimate factory. There was little noise from London and Tokyo, and America was the copycat waiting for trends to explode and make millions for the GDP.

What kind of a designer was I? I still find it hard to judge. I often tend to make light of my contributions. During those years, I collected enough awards, plaques, and good press to proudly display them. When I put women in pants the same season Yves Saint Laurent did, it was a big deal. The pages of *Cosmopolitan*, *Glamour*, *Mademoiselle*, and *McCall's* were stuffed with my work. *Harper's Bazaar* and *Vogue* were still turning their backs on this new upstart market. Although *Harper's Bazaar* started to wink in our direction. My pleated dresses appeared long before Mary McFadden found her *fach*. I was the talk of the industry and made companies like Vogue Pleating into grand success stories.

Everything I did was made in America, even the buttons and belts. Brooklyn was a foreign country for our factories. I also became famous for narrating my own showroom fashion shows. There was a cadre of new models, smaller, younger than the 550 girls—Renee, Tasha, Jenny, Barbara, Billie, and Beth Ann–that I booked every season. But the woman I fitted the clothes on was Bebe Winkler. I have always been loyal and tend to keep things in place for a long time. I felt change was disruptive and I kept building clothes on her aging body until she realized it was time and moved onto great success as a decorator.

People packed my showroom. Sometimes I think more for the show biz aspect than the clothes. They could also see them on the house model, but the era of models holding onto numbers and names that fluttered to the floor as they entered the showroom was long gone. The personality model was being anointed and a bit of color was peeking through. This was long before the leg-over-leg prance that we now see on the runway, not a smile in sight. Our girls were told to have fun, smile, and sell. And, boy, did they. Those days, the golden ring for any designer competing was the Coty Award. I had already received a special award, but the Designer of the Year award was the big prize. Eleanor Lambert, the most important publicist in the industry, had long ago discovered how to use the avenue to her advantage. She was a precursor to the Wintours of today. And although I had to share the big award with Anne Klein and Victor Joris, I did get my Coty statue in 1969, five years into our new Mr. Mort era.

This should have been the high point of my design life, a time to solidify and plan for the future, fill out the resume, and become a brand, but I didn't and the people who I surrounded myself also didn't. Russ Togs wanted greater growth. We wanted more exclusivity. The bottom line was beginning to bleed red ink and, so, too, typical of my work at the time, was the collection I designed for the Coty show which was based on lingerie to be worn outside. The press swooned. The stores were stuck with my shredding feather boas and bias satin slips. Rumors flew that we were going to close. I took out

COME TO THE ZOO
AND SEE
ALL THE LIVING ANIMALS
AND
LIFESTYLE 70's
BY
STAN HERMAN
MAY 12, 11:00 A.M.
BEER GARDEN
CENTRAL PARK ZOO
(AIN DATE - MAY 19 -11:00A.M.)
KEEP TICKET FOR
FOOD *

an ad in *Women's Wear Daily* denying that. We closed in 1970. Except for two attempts, one with Ben Shaw, entrepreneur to the star designers, and another with a replica of my early garmento days, I never went back to the Seventh Avenue Garment District as one of its designers. I have walked its rectangular grid many times since, but for business district meetings and fabric appointments, often looking up at the third floor corner windows of 498 Seventh Avenue, where I built a reputation as one of America's fast-charging designers or at 512 where I set the coat and suit business buzzing about my faux fur collection shown at the Central Park Zoo. Looking back at the balcony of 530 Seventh Avenue where I would slip out to have lunch on in the 1950s. These days it has lost much of its grubby working-class character that was smack up against the chiffon hemlines and fur-trimmed suits being artfully maneuvered on racks down the side streets. I still miss the old Metropolitan Opera House and Bill's restaurant, our very own Sardi's, but my memories still resonate—and how rich I feel for having had them.

FREELANCING

Although the 1960s had been my most successful decade, the 1970s were my most diversified as a designer and, in some ways, my most fertile time. I never caught on to the grunge of it all, but I did learn how to freelance and keep a business going. From that moment on, I was truly my own boss. Before Mr. Mort closed, I started a loungewear line by taking over a floundering giant, Van Raalte. I dug down deeply into the intimate apparel world that I am still a part of today. Diagonally east of the Garment Center, along Madison Avenue, was the home for intimate apparel, an industry that kept a very low profile. Most of the design companies were mom and pop operations, making good money, happy to be under the radar. Very few Seventh Avenue designers walked east to make their mark. I was one of the very few. It was my uncle, Sonny, who was an accountant for many of these companies, who introduced me to a firm, with the appropriate name, Slumbertogs, which anchored my presence in this very closely knit industry.

That Madison Avenue enclave is where I still live today, but most of the buildings are fast becoming furniture showrooms, and many of my friends, including Carole Hochman have left the area. They had represented the class of that avenue. Respect for design was their mantra. I now work with one of the seminal corporations that learned the art of big business and design, Komar. They too have gone to New Jersey where there are great views of the city and cheaper rents.

A true freelance operation needs a lot of customers and now, with loungewear set and

OPPOSITE Two icons standing in front of the original Bendel —Geraldine Stutz and Buster. I had a boutique in that store for almost two years, after my decade at Mr. Mort. We produced some of the most exciting clothes, but the dream ended abruptly, as often happens in our business, and I licked my wounds and moved on.

OVERLEAF Can you find me in this picture? I'm somewhere to the right, four rows back, just before I became CFDA president, as we were ready to spread our wings as an organization and produce the seminal 7th on Sale event. Camaraderie often goes hand-in-hand with tragedy.

DECEMBER 2

CFDA VOGUE

my faux fur collection causing stirs on the avenue, I was called by Geraldine Stutz to meet with her at Henri Bendel. Gerry was the most exciting thing to happen to brick and mortar and fashion. She had taken an old silk stocking operation and made it the place to shop. A series of boutiques within the store enticed the new young customer and their slightly snobbish buyers to set the fashion trends. But it was Gerry's bigger-than-life personality, head wrapped in a turban, that made it all happen. She had admired my work at Mr. Mort and asked would I like to design a line at Bendel, a line to be sold to other stores as well. There was one dress she kept referring to, a silver matte jersey swing, held to the body by long strings. I found out months later that it was the dress of choice of all the uptown 'ladies of the evening.' They had shortened it to crotch length and made them look like available ballerinas.

I was not the only designer at Bendel. They had a very young Ralph Lauren, the brilliant Stephen Burrows, and the exotic Giorgio di Sant'Angelo. But I was the only one with the showroom where competitive stores would come to buy Stan Herman for Bendel. The business lasted a little over a year. The two collections I did with my very special assistant, Bill Robinson, were brilliant. But there was trouble once again as there were too many fabrics, too much pattern making, and not enough personnel to make it work. Pat Tennent, one of their top executives, was in charge of my division, as she was of Stephen's. His lettuce-hemmed creations in one fabric were a perfect fit for them. My bias gabardine shirtwaist dress never did hang straight.

Gerry took me for a drink at the Monkey Bar. She was dressed for the theater in my double matte jersey shirts, black over white, and I was elegantly fired between the martini olives and my last swig of scotch.

The third component of my freelance world became my calling card to the 1970s and beyond—uniforms, a category seldom included in the world of fashion. By now, I had moved into the shabby but very elegant studio overlooking Bryant Park, a park that bares no resemblance to its current state. In fact, it was known as needle park and a great gay cruising ground. My assistant was a young man from Parsons, Carmello Pomodoro, as Bill Robinson had moved onto fame in the menswear market. Bill's short, brilliant career was eventually cut down at the knees by the AIDS epidemic. He was the sweetest of the lot. I was so happy for his success, and he remained a gentle giant as he faced the inevitable. Carmello was another matter—a beautiful illustrator, a beautiful boy with shifty eyes and a needy personality. He had talent that was often strengthened by other people's work. Success was his within two years after he had left me with my sketches and took a job with Charlotte Ford.

He too died of AIDS, having built an exciting business, never telling anyone he was sick. I spoke at both of their memorial services. Bill's was blanketed by the biggest snowstorm the city had seen in half a century. Too few people made it through the mountains of white, but those that did made it worthwhile. Carmello's service was at his showroom, heavily attended by the fashion A-list and the confused people who

worked for him, as their way of life was slipping away with their secretive boss' death. Included in the group at the service, was another ex-assistant of mine, Michael Ward, who worked for Carmello, a man of immense talent and discipline who could have easily taken over that business. Years later, I officiated at his wedding.

This all sounds like there were many assistants under every bush. Not true, but the studio was a great proving ground for their entrance into the business. Not quite the pressure of being on Seventh Avenue, but close enough to be a part of it. A few that stand out are Guy Culver, Pat Spratt, Lorenzo Deras, and Marc Jacobs, whom I hired when he was still in high school. And, of course, the one who has been with me these past two decades, Michael Schwarz, now my associate, who has kept this ancient mariner on course and viable way past my due date.

THE WORLD OF UNIFORMS

Uniforms were fast becoming my most important business in a country that doesn't like to be told it's wearing a uniform. It's not a badge of honor the way it is in Europe. My very first uniform design was for Avis Car Rental, which at that time was playing second fiddle to Hertz. Their headquarters were in Garden City, on Long Island, and their advertising agency was Benton & Bowles. I had done two Ban deodorant commercials for them while at Mr. Mort. That's probably why they came to me. Avis was rebranding and the president wanted a new uniform. They were a very red company —a great color, but too much of it goes a long way, especially when worn below the belt by the men who are still the largest part of their workforce and didn't want to play Santa Claus.

The president had the oddest request. He wanted a jacket that didn't have a button or a zipper, but would stay perfectly balanced during the workday. Today, jackets can have a crazy quilt of closures, but 45 years ago, order and formality were the norm in the uniform world. I put them in grey pants to offset their roadside red tops. The designer who designed Avis right after me was Halston. I believe he was the only named designer who took uniform designing seriously. Braniff Airlines was a good example of his work. Years later, he competed for Pan Am, the Holy Grail of airlines at that time. I couldn't make a pitch for them because I was TWA's and United's designer. So, I asked Edith Head to work with my manufacturer, Hart, Schaffner & Marks. She had always wanted to design an airline uniform and not for a movie. Those two in competition was pretty heady stuff, and he won, hands down. But in typical Halston fashion, he refused to shorten the skirts and dresses when asked by the airline. So Edith got the account and I am sorry to say Pan Am got the short end of the hemline.

OPPOSITE Two of my most seminal uniforms were earthbound: Amtrak and Acela. These sketches of the Acela uniform were designed to capture the sense of speed and efficiency of riding the train between Boston and Washington, DC. Even if the promise didn't always get you there on time, the ride was certainly smoother.

OVERLEAF This has to be one of my favorite uniform designs—a burst of color in the very brown 1970s. TWA was for me America's greatest airline, competing with Pan Am as the world's leading airline. These shirt jacks still seem modern, and the scarves were good enough to make it into the archives of the Smithsonian Institution in Washington, DC.

PAGES 88–89 JetBlue came into my world as a new airline with the name "Taxi." Well, they have taxied many runways with the name JetBlue, and I am still their designer of record, proud to be an initial part of their heritage.

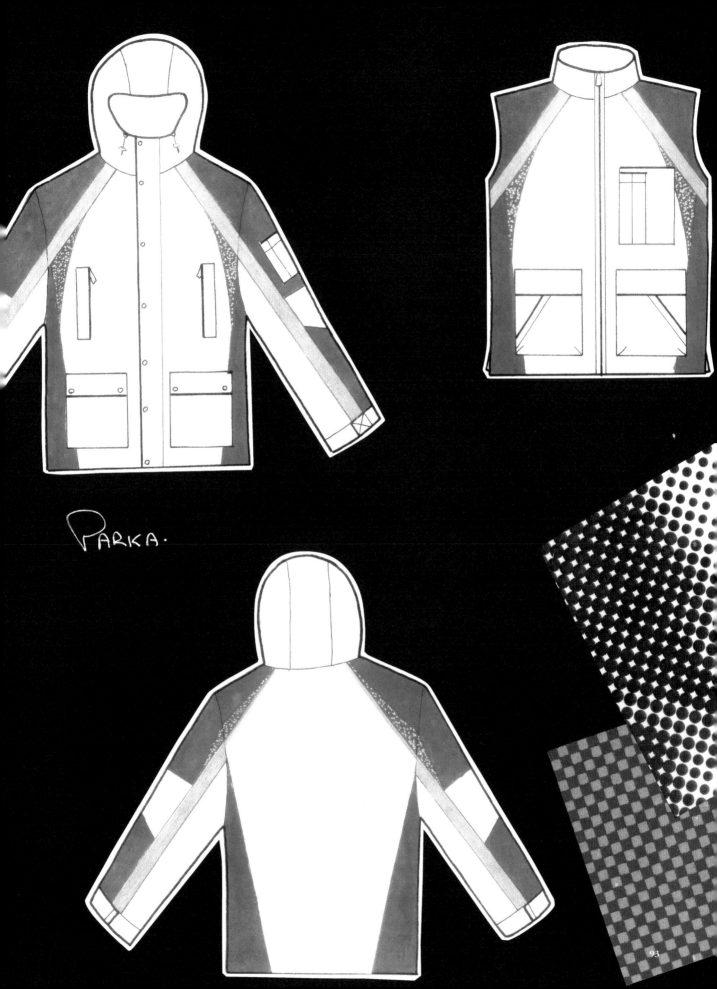

PARKA.

After 25 years as a ready-to-wear designer, I had found a new industry starving for design direction. There were other designers that were hired to entice large corporations but most of them tiptoed through the tulips, getting good money, lots of publicity, and were gone. At this point, I could have signed on with a manufacturer, probably making a fortune given the accounts I eventually won in competition, but I chose to be the freelance designer and not the manufacturer, allowing me to work with almost all of the companies, not limiting myself to just one.

In the next few decades, I had designed for the McDonald's Corporation, TWA, FedEx, United Airlines, Humana, Royal Caribbean Cruise Lines, Amtrak, Acela, MGM Grand, JetBlue and, now, the Central Park Conservancy and the Sandals Resorts. I still remain the go-to designer when uniforms are talked about even through the recent pandemic.

Three distinct worlds: ready-to-wear, intimate apparel, and uniforms. I found friends, families, and traditions in each one of them which made my design life so seductive. It's amazing that my studio thrived without a public relations agent. Clients seemed to pop up when needed, but to this day, I still don't have an agent and they haven't ever asked me. The studio still remains my sanctuary and, with Michael, I finally had an assistant for the ages. A young man from Idaho whom I hired the same day I met him. He has worked his brand of magic with both FedEx and JetBlue, the two accounts that I can proudly say have been with me—FedEx for over 40 years and JetBlue since they first started and called themselves Taxi.

The past 20 years have been a very innovative time to be designing uniforms. The search for fabrics that play with your consciousness, a time when gender identity is at play, and Americans are slowly accepting the uniform as a way of life. It's been a long time since I've put McDonald's in 100% polyester, their most iconic uniform that changed the way people viewed fast food clothing. At this moment, the studio is designing clothes for the Central Park Conservancy. What a wonder that this new uniform will be keeping that magnificent park well dressed. Better than looking at the markdown racks at Bloomingdale's. I am also designing for the elegant Sandals Resorts in the Caribbean.

I've just finished designing the clothes for the very high-profile TWA Hotel at Kennedy Airport, 45 years after I had designed the uniforms for that now-defunct airline. It's a hotel that sits next to JetBlue and is proudly displaying my old uniform in its magnificent Eero Saarinen Library. How wonderful that the circle of my uniform design is complete. At the official hotel opening, I was surrounded by all these loyal in-flight people who had kept my uniform for all those years, still proudly wearing the scarf, one of which is now displayed at the Smithsonian Institute in Washington, DC. Doesn't get much better than that.

PART II: THE INNER SANCTUM

I know we start and finish our lives alone, but to have found your soulmate makes the journey easier.

March 12, 1980

Dearest Stanley,

'Dearest Stanley' are the first two words ever typed on this, my newest typewriter. Every typewriter I have ever owned has been given to me by you. One might say that I owe my career as a writer to you; that is a truth true in many more ways than one. I owe more than half the years of my life to you. I hope to spend all the rest of my years making your years more joyous.

You have my admiration, respect, solicitude, ears, eyes, nose, throat, and,yes, indeed yes,

my love, _Gene_

Thank you for making everything in my life that matters, possible.

Thank you for making my 50th Birthday a genuine <u>birth</u>day.

And so, to proceed...

   Speak to me. Why do you never speak to me
   Speak....

Don't be afraid to speak to me.

Loving you has not made me fragile.

I love my new typewriter. I hope to write many, many, many books on it.

And so, to proceed...

GENE

It's about time I started talking about the most important person in my life. We met on July 25th, 1953, at 5:30 in the afternoon. I was at Fred Frederics' apartment, waiting in the wings for the orgy to start. One of the participants coming in from Los Angeles was late, so we all decided to go to a bar called William Tell on 54th Street. Just as we entered, I spotted a sunburned wisp of a man wearing a heavy tweed jacket and my life changed forever. It was at a time when, in a gay bar, one never touched one another. You never knew when the cops would be watching or the paid bartender would snitch on you. But I waved to him to follow me to the back of the bar and the minute we touched, there was no going back.

I told him I couldn't see him until the next day, but I would be home by 2 in the morning. He said he would wait, I gave him my telephone number and street address, which was the rooming house right off tony Fifth Avenue, near Central Park. I don't remember the details of the orgy, but I do remember that telephone ringing and sneaking him up past the landlady. I didn't go to work for the next two days. We never left that room.

So just eight months after my discharge from the army, while I was making up for lost-time sex, I suddenly hit the wall of contentment. I found the person who made sex with my own sex seem as natural as what I was taught heterosexual sex would be. He was the person I wanted to start building a life with.

A year into our relationship, we had just finished having great sex on a lazy afternoon. I remember the sun was shining through an open window; both of us had lit up cigarettes. I was a two-pack-a-day smoker in the spastic Bette Davis style; he, more Paul Henri, with long drags that produce an endless stream from every orifice. He turned to me and said, "I think we should split. I don't think you're ready for the same kind of commitment I am. I love you. I will wait for you. And when you feel like you can live with me without guilt or frustration, we will build a life."

I couldn't believe this was happening. As far as I was concerned, I was in love. In the year that we were together, I hadn't—I should say, almost hadn't—fucked around. I know I can be a knee-jerk flirt, but he was my guy, and I knew I would never feel this way with anyone else. I was devastated and confused. As it turned out, he was right. He took a big chance when he made that decision and he knew it. I was suddenly back on the market, nursing beer at the Village bar scene, leaning up against the meat rack on the western edge of Washington Square Park, following big baskets into the bushes, rediscovering the world of eye contact in *all the old familiar places.*

I quickly reintroduced myself to the gay underground. I found myself in the arms of some heavy hitters: Ellsworth Kelly, who was still in his Rembrandt period; Gore Vidal, who bedded and beheaded many; his sweetheart lover, Howard, who took singing

PREVIOUS PAGES This is my soulmate. You get what you see. And what you see is the man who gave meaning to the bulk of my life.

OPPOSITE The very day that I thought this memoir was complete, I was cleaning out my desk and this note, written to me on the typewriter I bought Gene for his 50th birthday, slipped to the floor. Make of it what you will, but it made me feel that the circle was complete.

**ABOVE AND
OPPOSITE** The two
of us wore the same
polo shirts the year
we met. The photo
may be faded, but
the sense of our
future together was
crystal clear.

lessons with me; the underestimated gay icon, Bernard Perlin, who had the most beautiful penis; and the one designer I had a fantasy crush on, Chuck Howard. We were mirror images of each other, which did not make for great sex.

Just about a year later, Gene came down into the city in his sea-foam DeSoto. It was a snowy Christmas Eve and my friend, Selma, had shamed me into seeing him again. When the buzzer rang and he walked up those four flights, by the time he reached the top landing, I knew my life would change. I lifted him into my short and strong arms and, soapbox as it may sound, that was the beginning of an extraordinary 40-year-long relationship.

Our sex was always good. My inability to totally let go often stopped it from being great. He was always ready, and often I was feeling guilty about the quickies I had had that week. For much of our life, after Gene stopped teaching, he would spend summers

in the Hamptons, which would leave me too much time to twist and turn, and avoid temptation. There was always his welcome arms when I came home. We were a couple that loved to dance together, very often changing roles during the dance. I wanted to lead. He would let that happen until I suddenly realized I was being led. He was the housekeeper, but never the Griselda. I was the provider who came home to the order he loved. He was a very sexy man. His smell was delicious and all of his large appendages provocative to me. From his nose to his toes, and everything in between, he was my type. To this day, I am stopped dead in my tracks by anyone who looks like him.

I am using terms that heterosexuals use in their relationships because we were a couple in that sense, but we didn't have road signs to follow. There were no written regulations to keep us together in the homosexual world. We had no pre-nups, no divorces, no children. It was just the two of us, surrounded by his understanding family and my

uncomfortable family. We built our life together gracefully. Much of that had to do with our friends. We were both working in professions we loved and, in truth, we were not hemmed in by restrictive rules and regulations. Gene and I became a poster couple in *The Advocate*, the gay magazine, at a time when they were looking for normalcy in relationships.

People constantly described our affair as inspirational. We just thought it was normal. After he died, quick sex became easier again. Even then I carried guilt with me for at least five years. It became my way of avoiding a serious relationship. Better a trucker looking for action, than someone to hold hands with at the opera. Better a butcher from Bohack's than shopping for fruit with a lover, or a fireman named Tom than party talk behind the Hampton hedges. Sex that always seemed available, and that I could conquer without obligation.

Over the years, there were a few that became steadies. If I had learned how to text, I would probably still be doing it. There were even a few who took it seriously. Some who even recognized me while watching QVC with their wives. I had become an artful car cruiser. Range Rovers attracted one type, Jeeps another. Even to this day, I have both and my cup runneth over.

Gene will continue to appear many more times in this memoir. He has touched almost every aspect of my life even 30 years after his death, which is very much like the first night I met him, when everything happened very quickly. He had a major heart attack at 6 in the morning and a massive one when plugged into the monitoring machines at Beth Israel Hospital later that day. The last time I saw him alive, he pleaded with me to go home and walk our dog, Mo. He said he was fine. The moment I got into the apartment, the phone rang and a woman's voice said, I better get back to the hospital quickly. Mr. Horowitz was not doing well. Mo was writhing on the floor, his body spasming from an epileptic attack. I dropped to my knees, cradling him in my arms, trying to stop him from choking on his tongue. I was forced to leave him, still fighting his way back, pleading with him to understand.

It is a short cab ride from my apartment to Beth Israel, but not short enough. When I got there, a young, well-muscled black woman swept me into her arms and took me into a padded room. Mr. Horowitz did not make it. I don't know how many people before me beat those walls in agony, but I beat them until I was exhausted. Reality took over and I started to reach out to friends and family. My man was gone. We were a married couple surrounded by a surprisingly supportive world, the centerpiece couple in his family, moving easily through the pothole fields of prejudice that gays often encountered. I always wonder if he let go when that second heart attack battered him, releasing me to a new life that swept me back into the competitive world of fashion. I will never know.

OPPOSITE Here we are on the dock that anchored our life in the 1960s. The picture of us with our friends, Michael Mahon and Chester Weinberg, was taken by Chester's lover, Michael Datoli, at the beginning of his photographic career—a quintessential 1960s picture with lots of hair and expectation.

OVERLEAF I bought this Missoni sweater for Gene when we were in Venice. It is one of the few pieces of clothing I kept after he died. It has kept me warm and fashionable for the past 30 years of my life, but he looked better in it than I do.

NOV 18 80
THE WRITER AT 6

THE WRITER

The 1980s were a confusing time for me. I felt hostility toward the Reagan era. I actively resented the fashion world cozying up to him. AIDS was dominating our lives and my career was taking a back seat to my home life with Gene. There was even talk of retiring. Both of us had settled into a comfortable living pattern, shuttling between the city and the Hamptons, surrounded by friends that were facing the *anschluss* of AIDS with us. We were becoming more political, more vocal, more radical, more deeply frustrated by our inability to stop the death spiral.

The times were more difficult for Gene than for me. His career was going nowhere. He was a fine writer, the author of five published books, all of them well reviewed. His first novel, *Home is Where You Start From*, almost became a runaway bestseller. Reviewed by the formidable Charles Jackson of Lost Weekend fame, in the *New York Times*. Norton, his publisher, was caught with demand and no product. Jackson called it the best family novel since Thomas Mann and the two of us were cloud-borne. His future as a serious novelist seemed set. My persuading him to stop teaching and become a full-time writer was a wise move, and the cadence of designer and writer as a twosome was poised to fill out a long life of accomplishments.

His second book, *A Catch in the Breath*, was inspired by our surrogate mother in Southampton, Revel Biggs. It was about her backstreet love affair and active sex life in her later years with the upstanding, churchgoing, town historian, Bill Dunwell. A book championed by the poet, May Sarton, who said it was the best book about an aging female she had ever read, but it didn't sell at all. I always thought it would have been a perfect vehicle for Bette Davis. Could have, would have, should have, but never happened.

And then Gene wrote me into his world of words. *Mr. Jack and the Greenstalks* was a novel about a bisexual designer. He felt the world wasn't ready to read about a gay designer yet. He was wrong. It was actually a book about big business in the fashion world and was well reviewed in the *San Francisco Chronicle*, calling it the best book about Seventh Avenue ever written. It did well enough to go into paperback and the deceptive title, Mr. Jack, sounded too much like a children's book, so Mr. Jack became the *Velvet Jungle*, and a big seller at airport bookstores.

Gene wasn't very kind to the Russ Togs family in the book, even though the names were changed. I was on a flight with Eli Rousso, the president of Russ Togs and watched him pick up a copy of the *Velvet Jungle*. Then I watched him toss it when he realized that Mr. Jack had reentered his life. The hardcover of the book was graced with artwork by my friend and superb illustrator, Jim McMullan. His posters for Lincoln Center have reached legendary status. I treasure our over half a century friendship. Gene and I named his daughter, Leigh. I even designed a little Mr. Mort dress for her

PREVIOUS PAGES There she is; Edie Windsor, the woman who turned gay rights on its ear, framed by the two of us. The dress she wears is one of my designs and she wore it throughout her long life. I love the comfort of this photo, I can still feel her presence.

OPPOSITE I must have drawn Gene hundreds of times. The pen is my camera. Here he is in Hawaii, leisurely writing in his journal after a long day. He wrote, I sketched, which was often followed by good sex.

OVERLEAF This is Gene's legacy wall in the guest room of my country house. I've framed all of his book covers and filled the entire room with his favorite books. It has aged well over the years and has watched many guests sleep contentedly at the lake's edge.

THE WRITER IN BUDDOCK JEANS

SEPT 15

birth. Jim's wife, Kate, says it is still folded away, not gathering dust, just memories. His fourth book, *Ladies of Levittown*, should have been a movie. Richard Marek published it to mild fanfare and waited to see if it would catch on. It was the story of the new suburbia and the friendship of a group of frustrated, politically savvy housewives, including one character based on his sister who participated in the writing group he taught. It's a very good book. It still takes space in the local libraries on the east coast. I know that there is still a copy at the Southampton Library. I finger it every so often. It was at this point in his career that he began writing books with a gay theme.

Cautiously at first, but with revolutionary abandon as the years flew by. None were published and he started to feel he'd lost touch as other writers were finding a home for their work. Andrew Holleran and Edmund White come to mind.

In *Privates*, his last published book, he succeeded and told the story of his time in the army and its gay underground. Published by St. Martin's Press, I believe after *Home* it was his best book. Long after he died, I paid a young man to write a screenplay of it and almost got a Hollywood agency to buy it. I may try again. It's so prescient today. Gene continued writing until the day he had that heart attack. Every morning, he cleared the table after he had a good breakfast, and wrote. He seldom wrote later in the day and treated it as if it was a 9-5 job. The weekends were reserved for us. There were times when he closed himself away completely and didn't come out for days, but that was rare. He spent months at the MacDowell writing colony breaking bread and sipping scotch with his fellow writers. He was working on a novel about Walt Whitman and his affair with the trainman Peter Doyle when he died. I tried to get a publisher interested. My friend Parker Ladd, Arnold Scaasi's partner, and a force in publishing, sent it to his contacts. They all said it needed more work and weren't interested in fluffing a dead author.

I have a closet filled with manuscripts fading away, all of those typewritten words turning to dust—his five published books anchoring the bookshelves in my study, beautifully leather bound by his publishers. There is a snapshot of him dressed in his serious hippie style, lounging comfortably at the lake's edge, staring directly into the camera I was holding, ready to face anything. There is no fading there. The colors of his clothes are still vivid, the glow of the lake still gleams. He looks confidently into the lens as if there were possibilities everywhere. After Gene died, I slept on his side of the bed for the rest of my life.

What happens when reality sinks in, when your partner is gone and mourning is an experience you can no longer deny? How do you cope with the fact that you're alone? That all those years you've been swimming with the tide and treading water together are gone and now there are all only memories and photographs to hold onto?

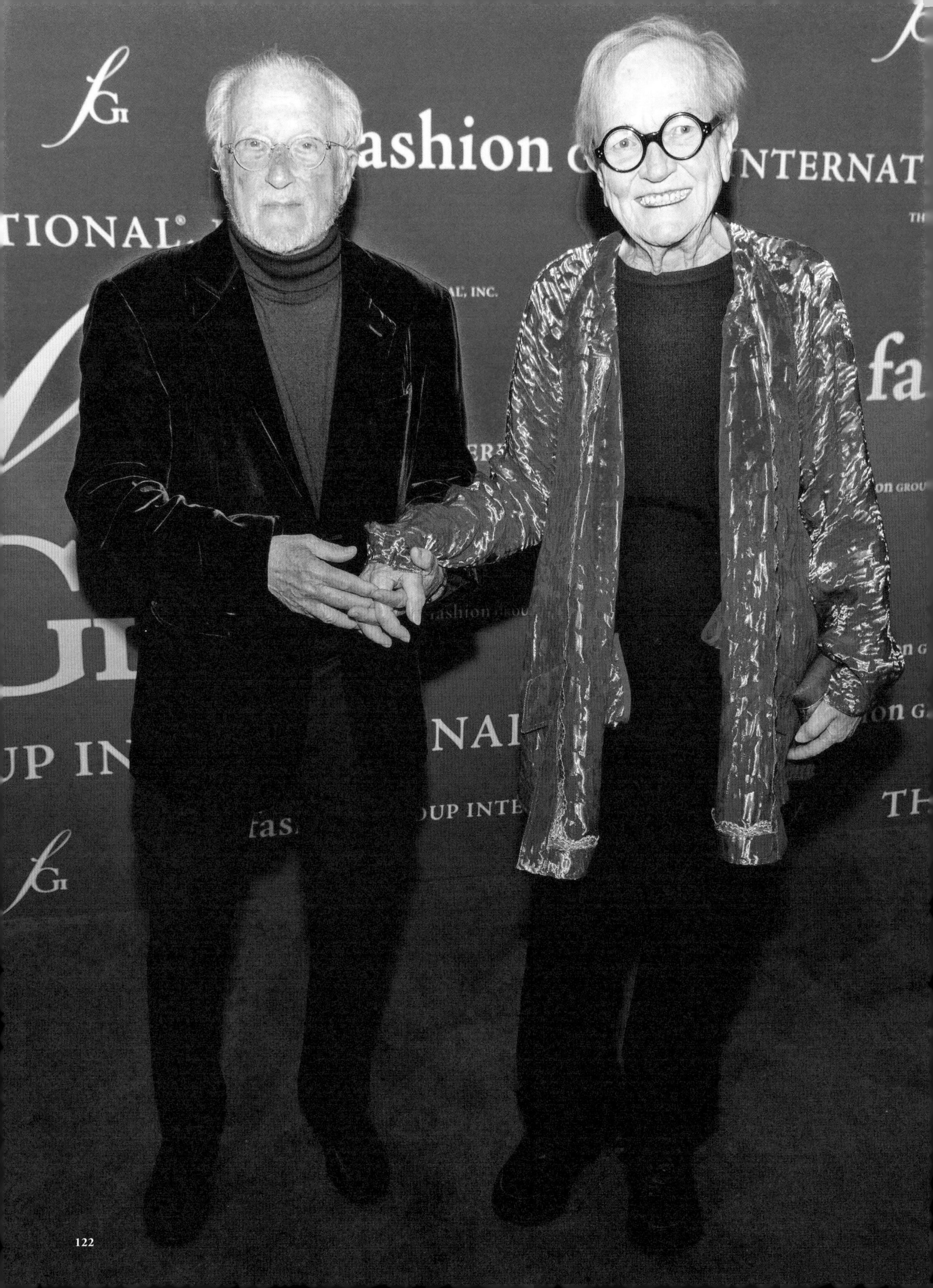
fashion

OUT OF THE SHADOWS

Suddenly, I was surrounded by well-wishers who had pulled me to shore, anointed me the president of the most prestigious organization in fashion. To many, I was a new face. To others, an old timer with a familiar name. There were calls from publicity agents, manufacturers, and designers I hadn't heard from in years. One particularly striking call was from Eleanor Lambert who, until the end of her life, held out the possibility that she would get the Council of Fashion Designers back under her aging wing. There were new friends like Fern Mallis and old friends like Marylou Luther who was waiting for me to come back to land.

I am sure Perry Ellis never knew that by putting me on the board of the Council of Fashion Designers of America, he changed my life forever. I had been an active member, quite vocal, for someone who had little power in the industry, and I was truly surprised when it happened. His tenure as president was short, but he, more than anyone until my presidency, changed the focus of the organization to be less elitist, more embracing. There was even a time in the 1960s that I couldn't get into the council. My clothing was too inexpensive and not *Vogue*-worthy. *Mademoiselle* and *Glamour* hadn't yet penetrated Eleanor's barricaded fortress of a council, but there was a definite youth movement, pushing for recognition. It was Perry Ellis with his oxford-blue shirt and belt-less khaki pants personality that led the charge.

At the time, all board member meetings were scripted and members were assigned specific parts. The motions were usually seconded by Mary McFadden. And when I spoke, my words were underlined in yellow. Everything was organized by Eleanor. She's the woman who is given credit for discovering the American designer. She controlled press week and used the council's prestige for her public relations business, an elegant midwestern lady who quickly realized how insecure designers were and took advantage of it. I give her lots of credit. She reigned supreme for almost half a century. To this day, I am part of a small group of designers who lunch in her honor, clinking a glass to her memory. One thing she never expected to happen was my ascendency to the presidency of her beloved organization. Her influence was already weakening when Perry appointed an executive director, Robert Raymond, questioning her role as publicist for Coty and controlling our gala, appropriately named the Coty Awards.

It was eventually Oscar de la Renta who spearheaded the split with Eleanor and removed her from control of the organization. We were moving through the late 1980s and the AIDS epidemic was decimating our design world. Perry was one of the first to go. It was also the Reagan era. I should say the Nancy era, when it came to fashion. And it was the de La Renta and Blass era and their ladies who lunch. The council was their restaurant. Oscar's charm and big personality easily controlled the benign board. When his term was up, he had his assistant of many years, Carolyne Roehm, anointed as our new president.

OPPOSITE There would be many more red-carpet moments after coming out of the shadows, but this one, with my dearest friend, the journalist Marylou Luther, has special meaning.

OVERLEAF The events of 9/11 changed our country, and the CFDA responded by trying to massage the world back to normal with an American view. From left, Carolyn Murphy, Oscar de La Renta, Donna Karan, and Tommy Hilfiger were photographed touching shoulders at a rally to support designers and retailers.

PAGES 126–127 Ringing the bell at Nasdaq along with Steven Kolb, our executive director at that time. Father would have loved it.

127

Who knew she would throw up her hands in frustration right after the council had produced a thrilling fundraiser for AIDS called "7th on Sale," spearheaded by Anna Wintour and Donna Karan, raising over five million dollars with no mechanism in place to dispense it to the proper organizations.

At this point, I don't think anyone expected Stan Herman to take on that presidency. But that possibility happened when, with Monika Tilley, one of America's premiere activewear designers and a friend, I was given the job of searching for the next executive director. It was a monumental task that kept me grounded in our new mission. As time went on, I began to believe that we could be an organization that could galvanize a long, moribund membership.

I had never met Fern Mallis, but at the end of a long list, her name was brought to me by my friend and designer, Jeffrey Banks, and the publicist, Mary Loving. Fern handled herself brilliantly before the board and was unanimously hired, which by the way was on her birthday. Once she was in place, the women I call my three angels, Patricia Underwood, Mary Ann Restivo, and my partner in the hiring process, Monika Tilley, had no problem convincing me that I was the natural choice for the presidency. The only stipulation I made was that I be elected unanimously, and I was. I believe Oscar was out of town.

We had five million dollars in the bank, money that was raised to support all of the young AIDS organizations popping up, most of them underfunded by federal and state organizations. I don't have to remind people of the government's reaction to the plague. Our own closeted mayor, Ed Koch, was no help. Fern went to work and a revitalized membership made my job easy.

The CFDA came to fundraising late in the game. Until this time, our treasury depended on the gala at New York's Metropolitan Museum of Art, and all the profits went back to the museum. It was a cozy relationship in a cozier time. What 7th on Sale did was to galvanize our membership, and the CFDA would never be the same. Sixteen years and a bottle of scotch. It is hard for me to believe how quickly the 16 years went by, how many bottles of scotch I consumed during my tenure, how many times I complained that there was no brown liquor at the parties and boy, did I inherit a luxurious first-name board: Oscar, Bill, Mary, Ralph, Calvin, Donna, Michael, Carolina, Vera, and Kenneth. In addition to my three angels and my friend Jeffrey Banks, our cup runneth over. There is nothing more exciting than a sleeping giant waking up happy, not like Siegfried's nemesis.

It's also amazing to look back at the original board—names like Norman Norell, Nettie Rosenstein, and Pauline Trigère. I believe there were 12 and, with Eleanor, they were the ones to bring the council to life, and anyone who had fashion credentials wanted to be a part of it. Sixteen years and a bottle of scotch, my drink of choice; 16 galas to plan; 16 new membership classes to vet; over 50 board meetings to plan for; and, over the years, three executive directors to work with: Fern, Peter Arnold, and

Steven Kolb. For almost 6,000 days, the council became my lover. Perfect timing after Gene's death.

Our new office at the council was quickly filling with bright young faces, many of whom have gone on to important careers in fashion—including Lisa Smilor who is still there, embracing membership with her body hugs. And Cassandra Diggs, who kept our organization financially solvent. Our first big move was to distribute the five million dollars raised at 7th on Sale to organizations like the Gay Men's Health Crisis, CRIA, and the Hetrick–Martin Institute. Eventually, we ended up giving the responsibility to the New York Community Trust, who dispersed our funds with great professionalism.

Next was to take the gala out of its cozy elegant space at the library and move it to the State Theater at Lincoln Center. We went overboard, hiring a show business producer, building sets, and searching for Big-Name presenters. Scotch flowed smoothly. The theme was to celebrate art and fashion. We expanded the invitation base and beckoned the industry to attend. Students from the design schools filled the balcony and we were thrilled with the audience response. But the very next day, *Women's Wear Daily* and Mr. De La Renta started their pushback, which lasted the full length of my term in office.

My relationship with *Women's Wear Daily* during my presidency was never easy. Patrick McCarthy, who was a mirror of his old boss, John Fairchild, felt more comfortable having lunch with Oscar and his courtiers. I was never able to find common ground. Initially, I was surprised by how much animosity existed. I'm not the best in a confrontational situation so it took me a while to learn how to protect myself and my role as president.

Fern became a target as well and still has some of the wounds to prove it. She'll be glad to tell you. Too many times I had refused to become deep throat when *Women's Wear* was going through their tabloid moment. There was one time when Teri Agins from *The Wall Street Journal* broke the story about underage models. All thumbs came down and my name disappeared from their pages for a good year. It is a different paper today and much better for it. Of course, there was the force of nature that was Anna Wintour.

There has never been anyone like her, arms crossed or uncrossed, her glasses on or off. During my 16 years as president of the CFDA, she became an important presence in our organization. From her perch at Condé Nast, she has ruled the fashion world. I didn't always agree with her methods, but I have a deep respect for her commitment. I was never the constant house guest, but the door was often opened.

There were many glorious nights. I think of some of the classiest dinners catered by Sean Driscoll of Glorious Food, and decor by Robert Isabell and Colin Cowie. In the beginning, our lead sponsor was the Hearst Corporation, and Randolph Hearst's newest wife, Veronica, began testing her fashion credentials by becoming involved

November 15, 2006

Dear Mr Herman.

On behalf of the residents of New York City, I commend your 16 years of service as president of the Council of Fashion Designers of America. From your world-renowned uniform designs to your incredible retail success as a designer of chenille robes and loungewear, your work has been both critically lauded for its savvy and pioneering aesthetic and admired by the everyday shopper

Yet, while you are known worldwide for your designs, it is your philanthropic work as president of CFDA that sets you apart. From Fashion Targets Breast Cancer to 7th on Sale to Fashion for America, you have helped to raise millions of dollars for such important causes as breast cancer, persons living with HIV/AIDS, and the victims of September 11, 2001   We hope you continue to give back to our community, which has already benefited so greatly from your exemplary efforts.

Few individuals have had such an enormous impact on New York's fashion industry The fall and spring fashion shows under the 7th on Sixth tents that you helped create play a significant part in the industry's New York City success story given their world-class reputation and the excitement they generate each year We are proud to salute your tremendous contributions to this $35 billion business in our City

Please accept my best wishes for continued success in your endeavors.

Sincerely,

Michael R. Bloomberg
Mayor

with the council. Probably the most glorious gala that we ever produced was the year Princess Diana came to give an award to her close friend, Liz Tilberis, of *Harper's Bazaar*. I still carry the image of this statuesque goddess, hair slicked back, peeking out from under her eyelids, charming the jaded fashion cognoscenti.

One of my favorite duties as president of the gala was to choose the food to be served. Veronica hated garlic so after we chose the menu, I would go back to Sean to tell him to put it in anyway. She never complained. There was one gala that we had decided to televise, an idea that had been floated many times by my predecessors. I remember Mary McFadden, being extremely excited by that possibility ten years before, as well as Tommy Hilfiger was, more recently. Fern and I spoke to every major channel. All seemed to show interest, but never came through until the year we decided to film it live. It was the year that we gave Yves Saint Laurent a major award, and everybody who was anybody paid top dollar to see the world's most famous living designer at the time. We even had a live fashion show by Yohji Yamamoto that went on forever.

Earlier that day, I had given a preview of the awards to John Fairchild, thinking that I had completely charmed him. Well, the show went on for four hours. Half the audience had left, including my complete table, and my bottle of scotch was empty. The review in the *New York Times* the next day by Cathy Horyn was devastating. I felt like pulling a Virginia Woolf, weighting myself down with rocks and wading into the lake, but my competitive personality was revived after I read Mr. Fairchild's description of me as "that bathrobe designer." I would go on to chair many more galas, and have proudly sold hundreds of thousands of my iconic bathrobes on QVC for 30 years.

LINE OF SUCCESSION

My presidency followed a long line of succession going back to 1962, the decade that my career flourished. It was the era of, "Do Your Own Thing." Well, I was doing it against the backdrop of a war that split the country, very much like what is happening today, 60 years later. The council was a fraternity of designers who masterminded the emergence of American fashion onto a global platform.

At this time, few people knew that Bill Blass was the designer of Maurice Rentner or that Norman Norell was the backbone of Teal Traina, but Eleanor, the visionary press agent of fashion, did, and she knew their frustrations and began to build a cohesive and better market in New York as well as forming the Council of Fashion Designers of America (CFDA).

Our first president was Sydney Wragge and the illustrious group included: Bill Blass, Donald Brooks, Betty Carol, Gene Derby, Luis Estevez, David Evins, Rudi Gernreich, Bud Kilpatrick, Helen Lee, Jean Louis, John Moore, Norman Norell, Sylvia Pedlar,

PREVIOUS PAGES
Heady stuff—
The Princess, Kay
Graham, Anna
Wintour, the back of
Ralph Lauren, and a
very happy me, in
Washington, DC.

OPPOSITE Every
time I read this
proclamation, I
realize how much
our industry is an
important supporter
of our city's reputation
and economy.
Michael Bloomberg
was a mayor who
truly recognized
our contributions.

OVERLEAF Two CFDA
presidents, one great
cause, and Mary
McFadden holding
her end of a very
heavy check.

Count Sarmi, Arnold Scaasi, Adele Simpson, Gustave Tassell, Pauline Trigère, and Ben Zuckerman. It's amazing how many of these people I actually knew and considered friends, all of them now gone.

In the beginning, the membership was extremely exclusive, with most of the designers being represented by Eleanor's agency. The world of fashion, or I should say Seventh Avenue, was dominated by very few. We had no French Chambre Syndicale to anoint us. The CFDA became our personal trainer and that exclusivity remained until the 1980s, when a wise Perry Ellis decided it was time to move on and make room for expansion.

Oscar was our most important Emperor. Hand-in-hand with Bill Blass and encouraged by Eleanor, he married us to the Metropolitan Museum of Art on Fifth Avenue and we danced the Viennese Waltz for three decades with them. Our gala every year was a benefit for the museum and our treasury remained undernourished, which did not prepare us for the windfall our 7th on Sale fundraising event produced.

There was a short presidency for Herbert Kasper, one of the first designers I met when I came to New York. I have to say I assumed that Mollie Parnis ran the show during his term, as he often used her office for our meetings.

When Mary McFadden became president, I remember her trying to get our gala televised. No one took her seriously. I attempted it disastrously, years later, and almost every other president has flirted with the idea ever since, including Thom Browne at this very moment.

Then there was the short, but volatile year that Carolyne Roehm was our president. She, at one point, was Oscar's assistant, and now he was anointing her to that position. She, along with Anna Wintour and Donna Karan, produced 7th on Sale, which suddenly fattened our treasury with enough money to become a leader in funding the fight against AIDS.

Thirty years later, I came out of nowhere to become the CFDA's longest term president. I was there at the right moment and had enough time on my hands to handle the complexities of an organization ripe for expansion. My horoscope predicted all of these changes and I let go and allowed them to happen, following my natural instincts to cope and conquer.

Our next president was the Empress, Diane von Furstenberg, and she fit the bill perfectly. With Stephen Kolb, she lifted our profile to global standards and she, too, was seduced into a long reign. Those galas flipped by very quickly. She made it difficult for anyone to follow in her well-heeled footprints.

We asked many to step into those shoes, but few would commit until Anna—it always seems to be Anna—twisted Tom Ford's well-manicured hand and the line continued. Tom probably didn't realize what he got himself into, but I'm glad that he did. A perfect illustration of how he works: I was waiting for a phone call from him at 3 pm sharp. Seven minutes after the hour, the phone rang and I said, "You're seven minutes late." Without a beat, he said, "No, just six." I think he's got it down, and he will

OPPOSITE She was the perfect pick to lead the revitalized CFDA, and was in her prime—Fern Mallis, who quickly became my fashion work wife.

OVERLEAF Diane, it's all yours, kid!

need every note in the song to keep the council functioning in these extraordinary times. He's asked me to be involved. I'm flattered and fully intend to work with him. I guess I'm now considered the *eminence grise.*

MUSIC AND AIDS

Before I became chair of the CFDA, everything was dominated by the AIDS epidemic. We were all dodging the bullet. Because of my relationship to Gene, my aversion to drugs and my sexual preference being oral rather than anal, I got through that decade in spite of my promiscuity. When Gene died, many people assumed it was AIDS. It wasn't. And immediately after he died, I got a serious case of the shingles. My country doctor in Southampton assumed the same. I never went back to her.

In the 1980s, I was the chair of the East End Gay Organization (EGGO), and, in 1985, I co-chaired the first AIDS fundraiser on Long Island at the home of *New York Times* food critic, Craig Claiborne, in East Hampton. It was the opera gala that same year, produced by Bob Jacobson, the editor and chief of *Opera News*, and Matthew Epstein, the opera guru, who made the Arts column of the *New York Times* that I am most proud of. We secured both young and established Metropolitan Opera stars to give us their high notes in the East Hampton gymnasium: Kathy Battle, Aprile Millo, Carol Vaness, James Morris—a special favorite of mine, Evelyn Lear, and the forever young, Roberta Peters, and, many more. We raised over $200,000. I still have the tape of the bravos that shook the walls of the auditorium.

All of this happened the day after the most devastating hurricane we had seen on the East End. The tents came down and our caterer, Ina Garten, then known as the Barefoot Contessa, had to start all over again. There was a glorious poster designed by my friend Paul Davis with an androgynous figure, arms extended to the heavens, calling into infinity. It perfectly summed up the mood of the time and every time I pass its well-framed presence in my home, I think of that stormy evening and those glorious voices that led me to a long relationship with the opera world. By the way, the emcee was the incredible Madeline Kahn, who could hold her own with any of the other singers' high notes.

I also chaired the Take-Off parties at the East Hampton airport, probably the biggest gay parties outside of Fire Island. Friends were dying and friends were waiting to die. There was no cure. At the same time, organizations were forming to raise funds that should have been forthcoming from the government. They say tragedy often inspires camaraderie. I believe that.

The first four Take-Off fundraisers were magical. In the first one, we sold about 50 tickets, hoping that the door sales would be big. Our headline act was a newcomer,

TAKEOFF 96
A BENEFIT DANCE PARTY FOR LIAAC

SATURDAY, JULY 27 8:00 PM TO 1:30 AM EAST HAMPTON AIRPORT A **LONG ISLAND ASSOCIATION FOR AIDS CARE** Production

Based on an **ROBERT KEILT** Music **FRANKIE KNUCKLES** of Def Mix Live musical **GROOVE COLLECTIVE** Event **STAN HERMAN**
original concept by   by   Productions performance by   Chairperson

Entertainment **EVENTS FX** Sound **G.S.A., NEW YORK** Tickets **JUNE 1** To order tickets and for ***CircuitTix*** **1-800-429-3433** or **LIAAC (516) 351-5777**
lighting system by   by   on sale   more information, call

Tickets are also **BOOKHAMPTON** locations **FIRST CLASS TICKETS** $200 includes admission to the First Class Lounge, Open Bar, **BUSINESS CLASS TICKETS** $85 includes Admission, Hors D'oeuvres,
available at all   Buffet Dinner, Late Night Show, Gift Bag and T-shirt   Open Bar all night, Late Night Show

For discount travel rates call American Airlines at 1-800-433-1790 and say Star# S 0476AG. Show your TAKE OFF wrist band at the doors of FLYING POINT in Southampton and THE SWAMP in East Hampton and receive free entrance to their AFTER PARTIES!

RuPaul. I believe it was his first big gig. We sold 900 seats at the door and Take-Off took off.

Music has always been a big part of my life—the human voice in particular. And after I had chaired the Music for Life event in the mid-1980s, I suddenly found myself surrounded by voices. The money that Bob Jacobson left in his will was put in my charge to support young opera singers. It was enough money to intrigue the Richard Tucker Foundation and I had no pretentions that I could dispense it myself. So the Jacobson Fund was folded into the Tucker Foundation, and for years we supported young singers. The auditions were held at the 92nd Street Y, as they still are today. There were so many days that I snuggled into the balcony and listened to some of the most thrilling voices I had ever heard. There is something about the clarity in a young voice when they are competing to be heard. Mature singers have other qualities, maybe even better high notes and deeper chest tones, but the true sound of a young singer, for me, can never be duplicated. Some of the greats came through those auditions: Renée Fleming and Susan Graham come to mind.

Frustrated singer that I was, I always wanted to test my high B-flat on that stage at the Y. A quarter of a century later, I had my chance when I was being interviewed by Fern on that very stage with a packed house of friends and legitimate ticket buyers, including my dearest friend, Bernadette Peters, in the front row. In my excitement, I forgot to sing. Later that night, when I was asked to sing at the after party at a restaurant across the street, I was very pleased to sustain a high B-flat from the aria, "Nessun Dorma."

Everywhere I turn in my life, there is music. One of my closest friends, Terrence McNally, was, until his death during the pandemic, my opera buddy. His name is synonymous with Maria Callas because of his wonderful plays, *Master Class* and *Lisbon Traviata*. For almost a half-century, we would dish the Saturday Met broadcast, massage the throats of our favorite singers and disagree on repertoire. His secret favorite, Bellini; mine, Berg. I still keep in touch with his husband, Tom Kirdahy, who has been lovingly massaging Terrence's legacy. Just today, they announced that his opera *Dead Man Walking* will open the 2023-2024 season at the New York Metropolitan Opera.

I went to Philadelphia to see the first performance at the tryout of *Master Class* with Zoe Caldwell as the great singer. She was an amazing presence who defied her short stature with a basso profundo chest voice. On the way back to our hotel, she asked me if she was wearing the right clothing. Would Ms. Callas approve? I said I had no idea how Ms. Callas would feel about her clothes, but I approved and felt that the simple black suit that she wore gave her the stature necessary to intimidate.

Singers are known to have bad taste in clothing, although the new generation seems willing to look into the right mirror these days. My very favorite singer was an English mezzo soprano, Janet Baker. She never sang opera in America, but she did give a concert every year at Carnegie Hall. It was like making a pilgrimage to Lourdes in France, kind of experience for Gene and me. We were devoted to her sound and soul,

OPPOSITE I chaired this event for many years, and it truly took off when a then unknown RuPaul took the stage.

so much so that I wrote her a fan letter and said that I would design her a concert gown at my expense. To my amazement, the next time she came to America, she had her husband call me and she came to my studio to discuss my offer.

Now, for people who are worshipers of certain entertainers, this was like seeing Judy Garland and Lady Gaga rolled into one. Good lord, Janet Baker in my studio. She told me she had no need for a concert gown, that she was being Dame'd by the Queen of England and would I make her a "daming suit." Now what the hell is a daming suit?

We agreed on the sketch that I did, but not the color. She was a Leo who liked bright colors and I saw her in mysterious pastels. The pastels won because I couldn't get the bright colors and I made her a three-piece salmon-colored matte jersey suit with a matching turban. With the leftover fabric, I threw in a little short-sleeved shirt and off it went. I didn't hear from her for months. I kept looking at the British papers to see if she had been Damed. She was, but I still didn't hear from her until, months later when I got the sweetest note. She didn't like the suit, but told me how much she loved the little shirt. It had become her gardening staple. We remained friends from afar and for years afterward, after each concert, I went backstage and the "daming suit" was never mentioned.

I talk about music a lot. I listen to music a lot. Music has helped me cope with life. These days Gustav Mahler has become my new lover. I've been reading a book on his life that is heavy enough to give me a hernia. Every time I open it, I travel back to the turn of the last century, walk with him to the Dolomites, wandering through the fields and rivers around Tolbach that he depicts so gloriously in his Alpine music.

I'm an unapologetic romantic, especially when Richard Strauss takes the baton. Richard Wagner, bastard that he was, can melt my heart. A Janaeck phrase sends shudders through my body. A Schubert lied can be food enough for days. And Mozart, well, I even named my standard poodle, Mozart. Mo, for short.

THE STANDARD

They get a bad rap. Often a bad color, pastel pink, baby blue, lots of powdered white, but they also got their name because they are "the Standard." I am talking about the standard poodle and specifically about my glorious black standard, Mozart, or Mo. Ask anyone who owns one and there is an immediate rush to gush and often a hesitant sigh to protect their reputation as the secret weapon of the canine world. Most people admit when they are confronted by the breed, that they are extraordinarily bright, even beautiful in their natural clip. Not that I particularly care. We poodle owners live a rich life, mated to our dogs.

Mo came into our lives in 1989. Gene had always wanted a big dog after having miniature poodles for 25 years. It all started when my boss Sylvan Rich, poodle fancier, had a liter that was not going to be given papers, as the mating was not seen by the proper officials. His bitch had been sent to be mated to her own kind but everyone felt that she had fallen for a cocker spaniel of some reputation. So, when the puppies arrived, he asked if we wanted one and although I had my heart set on a Kerry Blue terrier, this little bundle of temperament arrived looking more like a Cockerpoo and Liffey entered our lives with a dubious pedigree. As the months went by there was less Cocker and more Poodle. When she reached maturity, it was obvious that the Poodle had beaten the Cocker to it. And we had a very attractive miniature Poodle that would eventually have two litters, all pure breed, without papers. Poodles would remain an important part of our life for over 25 years.

But it was still the silhouette of the Standard that haunted this household and every time that I saw one, I would race over to its owner and ask about the breed. One morning I was looking out the windows of my office on 34th Street and this brilliant looking young Standard was prancing across Madison Avenue. I rushed down five flights of stairs and ran after this poor woman who almost had a heart attack as I caught up with her on Park Avenue but, like true Standard lovers, we bonded and she connected me to the inner sanctum of Standard Poodledom.

Through her connection, I contacted a breeder with a liter. He told me of a litter of five of which he had a male and a female left, Laura and Lily. When I asked about the two names being female, he said that Lily was a male, but he was so beautiful that he could not seem to call him Lancelot, his given L name. Without hesitation, we said Lily was ours; we want the gay dog. So, Lancelot became Lily, Lily Mozart, and Mozart Mo, to his friends.

Mozart lived for 16 years and seven months. Born October 8, 1988, a libra, he died in my arms on June 3, 2004. He was our dog for two years until Gene's death on January 10, 1991. He became my link to Gene for the next 12 years. He went everywhere with me. Our six-block walk to work was an adventure in how many people would admire his strut, his haughty air, his ability to fill space splendidly. He went to noone, unless he knew them well. He would look the other way when the kitschy-coos started. He loved sitting in the car and would make my trips to the island a pleasure. I even flirted with the law by having him sit at my side in the HOV lane. So human was his posture that I never got a ticket. As he got older, the back seat became his preference and I had to suffer the single man's traffic flow.

We slept together, napped together, walked the stunning shorelines together, swam in the lake together and ate together. He got poached chicken everyday with his wet food. I never understood dry food pellets that were probably better for him. He was not a big eater and knew that there was always something in my hand when he didn't eat. I kept him in what I called a T-cut: clean face, no beard to hide that gorgeous

OPPOSITE This picture anchors my life in the Hamptons: Miles of sand supporting two of the most important figures in my life, Gene and Mozart. I still talk to it and listen for all the answers.

OVERLEAF I wonder who's the alpha?

nose, clean body, full chest and legs. I think you can tell by the picture, taken when he was nine years old, what our relationship was about. He was the alpha that walked away with my heart and held tight until the very end; an end that I had complete control over.

He started to fail very quickly, even though he still looked majestic until the last few months. Twice, I almost lost him in the lake as dementia started to control his days. If I did not hold onto him in bed, he would flail around trying to get up on weakened back legs and would fall to the ground if I did not catch him.

My good doctor, Peter, eased me into the final decision and he came to the apartment to give Mo that lethal shot. My associate, Michael, hovered upstairs while I wailed unremittingly against life's inequities.

He is now in the lake, his ashes scattered with Gene's, where mine will also be. I watched them on the shorelines, their powdered grains refusing to disappear in the summer water and dissipate into the sand. I suddenly realized that the ash droppings had created the silhouette of a prancing poodle. There is a pine tree at the entrance to my house that I found at the local nursery. Its yellow tag reads Poodle Pine, and it gives me great comfort to watch it grow and grace my life.

VOICES

Voices have shaped my life. There is no instrument that equals its ability to bring me profound pleasure. Not the violin or the viola, a close second. There are a few notes in the French horn that can stop time for me, and the piano can make its mark. But it's the tone of the voice, either male or female, but usually the female, that gets the hairs up on the back of my neck.

The simple, untrained vibrato-less sound of a young voice can be astounding, the crooning microphoned pianissimo of the pop singer, even satisfying, the twang of a country singer's oblique approach to the note before landing on it, is pretty good stuff. But it's the operatic voice with its overtones and control that gets me every time.

In opera, there is little deviation from the written score. The singers must fastidiously follow the composer's notations. What differentiates them from one another are their sound and the way they manipulate the notes. And when you hear a familiar phrase sung by a distinctive voice, I believe even the composer would stop to listen. The fact that I studied voice for 15 years, while making a name for myself in the fashion world, certainly has a great deal to do with my obsession with that sound.

There are certain singers that have entered my private space and refuse to leave. My gaydar immediately fell in with the millions of people who love Judy Garland. Not just the songs she owned, but the way she owned them. The thrust of her middle voice

made you feel that the walls of her throat were sheltering that sound. Her ability to go into overdrive and take you with her sent me swooning.

People who have taken voice lessons know all about the break in the voice, that precarious bridge between head and chest. Serious teachers train the voice in different ways; some even go as far as using sticks to hold your tongue down and keep the flow. Other teachers tell you to think high and smell the roses while finding the thread of head, but they cannot give you a sound. You are born with that.

Once I found the operatic voice, there was no going back to the bleachers. The first classically trained voice that sent me to the hallowed ground was my dear Leone Rysaneck. She was my operatic Judy Garland. I first heard her when Gene dragged me kicking and screaming to a performance of *The Flying Dutchman* in 1960. A perfect voice it was not, but the sound she produced above the staff has been ringing in my ears ever since. Sometimes it would take her a few seconds to land on the tone, but who cares. She eventually got there. And when she moved beyond the G into the money tones, no one was more thrilling. Madame Rysaneck became my friend and, after Gene died, she was very comforting. There are a few pictures of the two of us on my wall in the downstairs bathroom in my apartment in the city. I often find myself talking to her, waiting for an answer.

I've already spoken about my love for the great English mezzo soprano, Janet Baker. I can sprawl on my big leather couch in the country and listen to her sing the Ruckert song for the thousandth time—each time, a delicious slice of life. As I write this, she is still alive and probably pruning the roses in her garden in Sussex, England.

There are singers currently finding their place in my private concert, singers who have that special sound. Sondra Radvanovsky, a throwback to the golden age of singers, who could control every note without it seeming difficult. The tenor, Jonas Kaufman, whom I've waited 70 years for, makes Wagner sound as lyrical as Puccini—and his looks are certainly an asset. I see him every day on the home page of my computer.

There is a list of singers, mostly operatic, who have brought me to my knees. Voices from the past like Victoria de los Angeles, Lotte Lehman, Eleanor Steber, Jussi Bjorling, and Fritz Wunderlicht come to mind. Then, others that have the great money tones like Nilson, Corelli and Leontyne Price. I would pay top dollar to hear them any time.

There have been a few showbiz singers that have earned my attention, but the one who has become one of my closest friends is Bernadette Peters. One note and you know it's her; one song, and you're hooked. The fact that she is so nice and so beautiful in every way doesn't hurt, either. Bernadette sang for me when I received the CFDA lifetime achievement award then again, a happy birthday when I hit 90 and was surrounded by all my designer friends at Donna Karan's house. She doesn't know it, but I want her rendition of the song, Move on, from *Sunday in the Park* to be sung at the memorial service that someone will one day hold for me.

OPPOSITE The sound of her voice changed my life. I became an opera junkie and a voice fanatic: Leonie Rysanek, who sang at The Metropolitan Opera for over 40 years is legendary, and more importantly, she became my friend.

OVERLEAF LEFT Two posters from the Old Met watch over me in my New York apartment. They don't make them like this anymore.

OVERLEAF RIGHT Leonie, thinking about those "money notes" that have remained with me all these years.

I sometimes wonder how much people who do not like or have never been exposed to classical music have missed and how much better off the world would be if people would take the time to sit through a long concert. I believe it would take the edge off their ignorance and expose them to the wonders that people can achieve. It's hard for me to think of Donald Trump sitting through a Beethoven sonata, but I believe Barack Obama would, and he'd even enjoy it.

Many, many years ago, I choreographed a fashion show of my intimate apparel line. We showed it at Circle in the Square and I had all the models walk and dance to Ravel, Stravinsky, and Aaron Copland. It was one of the high points of my career, but not one store came and the fashion press was sparse. Those who did come saw Iman during her first month in America, circling and floating in layers of nylon tricot.

My ears always perk up at fashion shows when designers choose classical music rather than the thump and thunder that uncross your legs seems to inspire. Even the collections appear more important when Bernstein walks them down the runway or Schubert holds their hands while they make the turn. Add the strings and the brass, the beat of the timpani, and the designer's voice seems clearer to me.

PROBING

As I write this memoir, I keep probing, looking for the signs that led me to this long and eventually satisfying career. I hear so many designers talk of their mothers, grandmothers, and fashionable aunts who influenced their early interest in fashion. I can't say I ever wanted to dress anyone in my family except my stepmother who, I have to admit, could have been a clotheshorse. I never wanted to cut into rolls of fabric in Herman's silk shop or befriend those leggy ladies in our pattern library at the store. And yet, it had to have been those pattern books that inspired me to start sketching, and my mother's innate good taste. To this day, I am happiest with pen in hand, and I have become very good at it.

I can feel the fabric with a stroke; see the proportions with another stroke. Clothing becomes a picture to me and I've inspired my assistants to bring life to those dimensions. I believe there are many other designers who, like Karl Lagerfeld, sketch first. I see his work as pretty pictures for Chanel. Whereas I would hazard a guess that Cristobal Balenciaga and Christian Dior worked in fabric. The French designer I had a secret crush on was Jacques Fath. I think his big bows got to me. I seldom intellectualized my designs. It was only through Gene that I placed them in the Zeitgeist.

Looking back at my work at Mr. Mort, I can see the charm of my proportions and my tasteful sense of color. There were some very special moments. When I put pants under dresses and found the pleating machines that dotted the New Jersey Palisades, I was

157

ahead of the trend. But for the most part, I was working in the commercial lane, but with enough flair to excite the buyers and the press.

Even today, my work on QVC has kept my design juices flowing. I believe my sketches are even better now than they were years ago. To this day, I wonder why I never kept a good record of my work, a diary of life in design. It would have been helpful in writing this memoir. Was I not proud? I've kept lots of old books and vinyl records. My career in ready-to-wear was much shorter than my uniform business and my intimate apparel world, but I realize that without that dizzying decade as a hot young designer on Seventh Avenue, nothing else would have happened.

And what a decade it was: The 1960s, my moment in the hot crater. It was the: "Do your own thing" era. There was a new young fashion market, airborne with pot and expectations. The young designers I marched with were my dear friend, Leo Narducci, Gayle Kirkpatrick, Luba, Don Simonelli, Victor Joris, Betty Carol, Deanna Littell, Carol Horn, and Liz Claiborne. There were others, too, long forgotten. The graveyard of fashion could easily fill the hillside of Queens with their tombstones.

Ready-to-wear was my moment and nothing could have happened without the woman who became my muse, Barbara Larson, a graduate of Parsons, and her buddy, Joel Schumacher, who went on to Hollywood fame. She was the assistant of my life in 1965. She was not only talented, but a great beauty who wore clothes and discarded them quickly to move onto the next challenge. She was so good I began to depend on her and step back. And once the assistant thinks that they are responsible for the designer's success, they have to move on or remain subservient. She moved on and I rediscovered my mojo. There were others like the extraordinary Jan Johnson, a true talent who could've become the greatest accessory designer of the decade.

Between 1965 and 1972, I was airborne. Magazines spread their legs and let me in. Stores clamored for my merchandise. I was on everyone's guest list for five years, traveling the country, doing shows in every A-list specialty store across the country. I had the very first young designer boutique at Saks Fifth Avenue, which I overstocked and lost within a year. I won awards, little plaques and tablets that grace my house in the country and are catching dust in my apartment in New York City. I can remember when Nordstrom was a regional shoe store with a reputation for taking merchandise back. I loved doing shows in towns like Shreveport, Richmond, Pittsburgh, Denver, San Antonio—so many stores to choose from. In addition to all this success, I had a solid love life that overpowered my desire to be out there with the shiny people. I had business partners who did not think of the big picture. If they did, they never told me. It was me who should have made the next move and I didn't. I used to wonder if my promiscuity was one of the reasons I never became a household name. Too much energy fucking and dodging the consequences, not enough schmoozing in the air-kiss world of fashion.

At this point, I believe it is important for me to come to terms with my promiscuous

OPPOSITE The building on the corner of 40th Street and Fifth Avenue, whose top floors were occupied by *Vogue Patterns* in the 1940s. It was on those top floors that my career started. Today, my studio anchors the building on 40th and Sixth. There must be something happening there.

OPPOSITE These patterns are almost 60 years old...With a few tweaks, they could be worn with confidence today.

OVERLEAF LEFT My friend, Arnold Scaasi convinced famed sculptor Ernest Trova to design our industry's 'Oscar.' I believe the contorted silhouette represents the constant changing of fashion. Winning one signifies the pinnacle of achievement in one's design career.

sex life that I so neatly tucked under the covers. For a guy who was married in the true sense to one man for almost 40 years, a guy who, to this day, measures everyone in terms of that man's attributes, I never got over my need for sex outside our relationship —quick, anonymous, no-touch sex. I had a designer friend, Chester Weinberg, who knew that side of me and tried to entice me, pre-AIDS, into a full-blown operatic production of sex. Gene saw it coming and gently massaged me back to reality. He knew. He always knew. He predicted the AIDS epidemic, screaming at Chester that he was going to kill himself with sex, and he did. I believe my guilt kept me from using this chosen time to enhance my future in fashion. Now, nearing the end of my life, pounding on 95, anonymous sex still sounds intriguing, and for all those legs I've managed to uncross, I carry no shame.

Very Easy Vogue

AMERICAN DESIGNER ORIGINAL

Stan Herman

2039

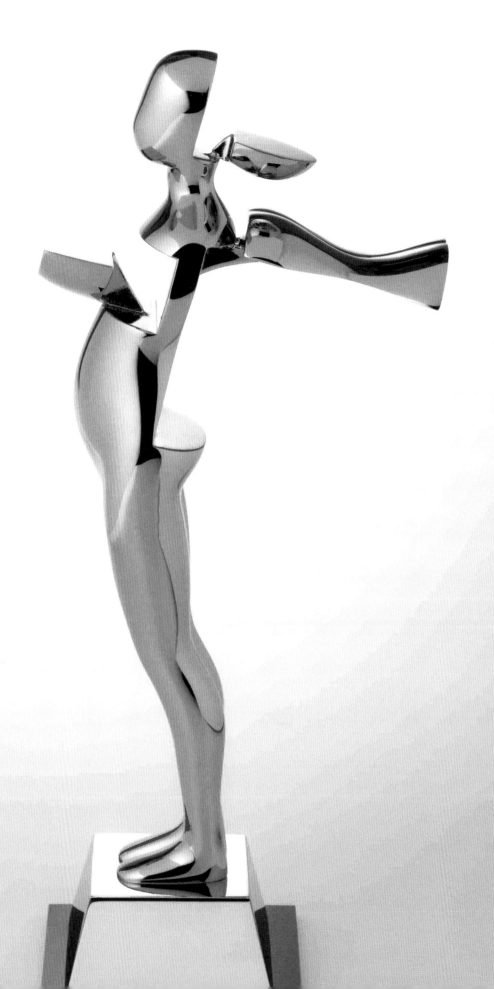

PART III: THE HOT CENTER

Biting off the edges has made my moments in the hot center of fashion possible.
I am in awe of those who flourish in the waves of the center's heat.

TENT STORIES

"Uncross your legs"—the call from the darkened room to get those privileged first-row power players to clear the sight lines. The title of this memoir deserves a chapter on its own. I wish I had kept a diary chronicling the years I was president of *7th on Sixth*. I suppose I could ask Fern. She could rat-a-tat-tat events better than anyone I know. When I look back, I realize the responsibility of being both the president of the CFDA as well as president of the fashion shows in Bryant Park was enormous, and yet, I did it, while running my own business out of my studio overlooking the same park that would become synonymous with fashion.

To this day, I often hear tourists walking along 40th Street, describing this perfect rectangle, plunked in the middle of Manhattan, as Fashion Park. I am still very active on the business improvement development board (BID) of Bryant Park, working alongside my friend, Dan Biederman, the quintessential BID president in New York. He made the park a place to stop time, to bird watch, to sprawl on its gracious lawn, to marvel at the heart and grace of its London plane trees. One of my greatest pleasures is to watch the workers in their Stan Herman uniforms, as I walk its gracious alleys, have my early morning breakfast, and secretly feed the 40th Street sparrows.

"Uncross your legs!" The first time I heard it was in the second year of the fashion shows. That was the year we built our tents on the two plazas of the park. It came from one particular photographer, Richie Renda, but after a while it became the clarion call from every one of the photographers who were standing on their postage-sized stamp on the edge of the runway. Somewhere in my files there are sketches of those crossed legs, those well-turned ankles, and the flat-footed men with their sensible shoes side by side with the elaborate sneakers and hairless bare ankles of their gay counterparts. After a while, I started to fixate on the bags that nestled between their legs. My legs being so short, it was usually my Prada man-bag that slithered into the sight lines.

These days the era of the iPhone and tablet have changed the rules of the game, everyone holding their phones, blocking your front-row view. A new expletive from the gallery of photographers might be needed, "Drop the fucking phones!"

In the beginning, there was always a front-row seat at the end of the runway set aside for me, next to Fern. She was at every show. That was her job. I still had a business to run because my presidential position was honorary. There were four venues in the park and many more within striking distance of the park's perimeter. Hotels began to spring up around the park. Rents in the area blossomed and the term "destination" was anointed. The eventual elephant in the room was the fact that this was a people's park and when the American designers decided to show before the Paris shows, we found the New York shows scheduled in the middle of Labor Day and that shiny satin bow began to unravel.

Now that the park no longer houses the shows and its relevance there is being questioned, it has found its own personality and I feel so privileged to still be a part of it, but I will never feel airborne in the same way again. It is the landmark Beaux-Arts building on the corner of 40th Street and Sixth Avenue that I have been in since 1975 that keeps me close to the hot center and is now surrounded by buildings that house some of our most prestigious names in fashion.

The tents themselves had names like Gertrude, named after the statue of Gertrude Stein, and Celeste, after Celeste Bartos. They were connected by carpeted hallways that sprung out from the glorious fountain on its western edge, a fountain that we stilled for the duration of the shows. In the very beginning, there was limited sponsorship so that the entrance became fashion-centric, especially the posers who lined up along Sixth Avenue. Eventually, the sponsors took over. You might have felt you were in a Mercedes or General Motors showroom. It was a necessary evil to support the shows.

I called the first few venues Bar Mitzvah tents. They had a catered affair look about them with poles that confused and blocked the sight lines. I remember the spring daffodils pushing up from the earth around the PortoSans, the electrical wires snaking in from 40th Street. But by the next year, it all came together and, once seated, no matter in which venue, the outside world disappeared and the fantasy world of fashion took over.

When you build a city—and the tents were a city—you have to have the right security. When we hired Ty Yorio and his company, The Citadel, we found a friendly force that was so good they are still watching over the fashion shows today. They were able to massage the large egos running around those halls and made me feel very special with their bruising hugs whenever we greeted each other. There is a picture taken of me with the whole crew when we moved up to Lincoln Center and, although I was no longer president, I still felt very much a part of that world.

So many shows, yet so few still resonate for me today. There was Isaac Mizrahi, turning the tables on the audience, letting them look behind the scrim into the models' dressing room. Often, you walked out of his shows admiring the productions and forgetting the clothes. Although I must say, his high-waisted suit silhouettes still look modern to me, and his recent retrospective at the Jewish Museum stripped away the artifice and exposed his prodigious talent. He is a wonder on QVC these days.

I have cried at a fashion show only once and that was at Ralph Rucci. Mr. Rucci is the last of the American couturiers. For me, his clothes capture the illusive quality of fantasy and reality. Just following the seaming that shapes the fabric into its silhouette is a wondrous journey. In the show that I remember, I was sitting in the first seat as the models entered and I could see them preparing for their walk down the runway— hushed, often eyes closed, a slight twitch in their torso, and out they came, one after the other—the world of Rucci on display. I suddenly felt my body go limp and the

shudder became a sob and the sob produced tears I had never experienced before. I told that to Ralph backstage afterward and he said, "Oh, I am often told that happens at my shows."

The largest tent held over 1,000 people, with standing room. In the beginning, the walls were white and when Donna Karan saw the venue, she wanted it black. She even covered the chairs in black. Suddenly word came down that she had changed her mind. Everything had to be white. And there were lots of people running around trying to make that happen. More importantly, the clothes were sensational. She was fast becoming the talent her mother told me she would be many years before. Looking back at her glorious decades in fashion makes me miss her voluptuous female clothing more than ever now that she is no longer in business. When she was building her Seven Easy Pieces that sent her on this stratospheric journey, she rented a studio next to me at 80 West 40th Street. Every so often, the door was open, exposing her design laboratory. Yenta that I can be, I often peeked in and watched what would be the origins of the way people dress today.

The most political of all the designers was Kenneth Cole. Before each of his shows, he telegraphed a message that tackled world problems. He was easily the political quarterback of our industry, and he used The Tents very well. If the clothes never quite reached the golden ring, it was always a good ride.

Another designer who knew how to work The Tents was Tracy Reese. The goodwill that flowed from her overstuffed venue was infectious. I never left a show of hers disgruntled and I could be very opinionated when I was disappointed. Often, I found my head falling into my chest looking at all those uncrossed legs. We now both live in the same apartment building and goodwill seems to follow her everywhere.

Nicole Miller was one of our mainstay designers. With her partner, Bud Konheim, they gave a special glow to their garmento DNA. The two of them seemed to balance the old and the new, by moving their showroom shows onto the runway. She seldom moved the needle, but inspired a devoted, dedicated following. To this day, long after my presidential credentials have expired, there is always a front-row seat waiting for this aging gentleman, and I enjoy the privilege.

I believe one of the most underrated designers in America is Anna Sui. Her shows at The Tents were a must for me. She always used the large venue and filled it with a joyful march into fashion. She made fussy simple and never, ever deviated from her vision.

I stopped counting the cartwheels that Betsey Johnson flipped at the end of her Hells-a-Popping shows. She would often reconfigure the runway to emulate a nightclub setting. Sipping champagne through a straw was good preparation for her special world vision.

The best cartwheel I ever saw her do was at her house in the Hamptons. After a casual presentation in her garden, she suddenly appeared and, using the edge of the pool, did a perfect cartwheel over the floating balloons and into its deep end. When she finally

OPPOSITE I never saw Joseph Abboud in any other color palette. He built an empire on shades of brown, and a career that transcends time.

OVERLEAF I peeked into the studio that Donna Karan was working in and watched her develop the landmark Seven Easy Pieces that would change the way women dressed. Her mother told me that her daughter would be famous one day. Never underestimate *Die Mutter.*

surfaced with those golden dreadlocks perfectly in place, it symbolized for me her extraordinary longevity in this industry.

And for the ladies who lunch, The Tents were their last hoorah. The shows at The Plaza, The Pierre, The Sherry Netherland—their comfort zones—were now being replaced by The Tents. They were now seated in section C at Oscar or Bill's show, nodding to each other as the tents filled with press and power and the eager standees waited to spot an empty space. There was no lunch in sight.

I think Bill had the advantage here. Being about ten years older than Oscar, he had sealed the deal quickly. Between his trunk shows and famous east side British accent, Mr. Blass had already perfected his art, long before Oscar began to muscle in. Although Oscar's calling card became his second wife, the formidable Annette De La Renta, I often sat directly across from that section, until the invites stopped and I used my position as president of the shows to muscle in. My favorite lady was the pom-pom puffed Judy Peabody, a wonderful woman in any venue. I don't believe any one of those ladies was bigger than a size 6 or maybe it was just the camouflage of their well-cut suits.

Going to Diane von Furstenberg's show was like attending a Broadway opening—less wiggle room for backsides, more celebrities per square inch, and the kiss-kiss gesture. I always liked Diane's clothes better in her showroom with their sensible nature that was often hidden by the razzmatazz of the stylists who have conquered the runways. And there was the Hollywood legend, Bob Mackie, whose career has long outlasted his sell-by date. He worked his special magic in one of those tents. Seventh Avenue was not his design home and I don't believe his strongest suit. But once he pushed those models out onto the runway, the magic dust was apparent. And at the end of the show, the audience was on its feet, including some of the toughest critics in New York. I now see him when we are waiting to go on camera at QVC, two survivors in the twilight of our careers, working it, working it.

When celebrities who felt they had fashion credentials discovered The Tents, it became a different experience. The first one who used The Tents well was P. Diddy. I think that's what he called himself then. And it was a very skeptical Stan Herman who went to judge him. The doorman in my apartment building begged me to get him into the P. Diddy show. He was an avid fan and loved fashion. I should have known better. Once I was seated, he disappeared. I was completely blindsided by the collection. Not the clothes as much as the attitude, a strut through the fantasy world of the new formula for the African-American lifestyle, model after model shining from head to toe, confident and bigger than life. Suddenly, I spotted my doorman on the runway, surrounded by the finale of models, waving at the crowd, smiling at me. He had finally found his home and he would never be the same.

Then there was the special talent of Han Feng, an Asian designer who did her first show in the smallest venue in The Tents. I didn't know her or her work, but I was told

she was someone to watch. Once again, I was blindsided. I was pulled into her world of wonder. I couldn't describe the clothes I saw. I don't remember them as individual pieces. I became so excited that when Han was walking down the runway, I jumped from my seat and wrapped her in a congratulatory hug. She freaked and I freaked, and a friendship was formed. She's no longer in our business, but she went on to conquer the Metropolitan Opera with her clothes for Anthony Minghella's production of *Madame Butterfly* and spends much of her time continent hopping.

For me, the designer who used The Tents perfectly was Michael Kors. With a touch of glossy packaging and glitzy lighting, he conquered the world, just waves of models working the runway, male and female. Every collection wasn't a winner, but every collection won me over. He is a throwback to the wondrous mom and pop labels that were the backbone of our young industry. To this day, his strut has defined American fashion, his personality the heartbeat of the glorious garmento world. He never left those roots, but his garden grew way beyond the confines of those times. Just watching Carmen drag her khaki football field-length cashmere scarf down the runway, says it all for me.

And, of course, there was, and still is, the extraordinary: Ralph Lauren. In the beginning, he showed in The Tents like all the other designers and generated the buzz that was necessary to keep The Tents relevant. Unfortunately, he found his own space downtown and built it to his personal specifications. It started a rush to leave The Tents by many high-profile designers who felt the need to do their own thing. But in the beginning, Ralph was our jewel in the crown. I remember sitting with our photographers in the trough below the elevated runway, watching every perfectly styled model glide down that runway. No fashion barriers were broken, but you walked out of the shows feeling confident that there were better days ahead, as long as he was around.

At this point, I think something should be said about the many designers who chose not to show in The Tents. I believe they missed out on the camaraderie that comes only when we all work it together. That moment in American fashion history will probably never be duplicated. The press world was constantly saying how great it was that we found a home for the shows only to mumble about having to shuttle between The Tents and those designers that chose to go it on their own.

Most of the big name designers showed with us, many eventually finding their own personalized venues. We gave a platform to the long list of talented designers who would never have been a part of press week. Most important, we nurtured many young designers by making those runways affordable. For me, Bryant Park was the perfect setting, just the right size at the right time. Eventually, there was talk about The Tents being too commercial. I'll buy that, but their contribution to New York as a world-class fashion destination more than made up for their loss of intimacy and exclusivity.

The last show I saw at The Tents was Tommy Hilfiger's—standing room only in the big tent—seated next to Fern. At the very end of the show, Tommy took the microphone and in his simple, straightforward manner, thanked us for our pioneering efforts. It's a gesture that I will never forget, a perfect ending to my ten-year run.

GARMENTO

During that ten-year term as president of *7th on Sixth* and the fashion shows in Bryant Park, I participated in a number of documentary films. The first was called, appropriately, *The Tents*. It followed Fern and I through the process of forming those fledgling press weeks and setting our tents up in that elegant city park. But when I was approached to be part of a film called *Schmatta: Rags to Riches*, all of my garmento personality kicked in.

I've always felt protective about that word. My father owned the biggest *schmatta* store in all of New Jersey. I knew what a rag was from the time I was a toddler. My instincts about the film were right. It turned out to be beautifully produced, directed, and championed by the formidable Sheila Nevins. I came off well, aging sage that I've become, with lots of history in this head. My face-off with the Russ Togs conglomerate fashion versus commerce is a story often told. They closed Mr. Mort because no matter how much the press genuflected, the bottom line didn't support the applause. At the same time, they were exposing their dubious business practices, which a conglomerate often uses to improve the bottom line.

The film artfully showed the chipping away of manufacturing in America, especially in New York with the loss of the mom-and-pop accessory companies that lined the Garment Center side streets, the shuttered, often antiquated factories that sewed so much of America's finest fashion labels, and the gentrification of the buildings lining Seventh Avenue and Broadway, where showrooms were giving way to law firms and insurance companies, where every move meant rent hikes that made staying within what I called the campus no longer affordable for manufacturing. The rush to produce along the Asian rim and compete for fast fashion at the lowest price left a void that would never again be filled, all of this to a pulsating performance of George Gershwin's "Rhapsody in Blue," a score that pumped up expectations and at the same time succumbed to the inevitable. Since the film, the Garment Center has opened its arms to a phalanx of hotels, 50 and counting, restaurants that never saw an egg cream, and a coffee shop on almost every corner to keep the adrenaline pulsating. There are happy hour bars that, until the pandemic hit, made sex after work easily available.

I've spent many years as a political activist in the city. Back in the 1970s, Mayor Lindsay put me on Community Board 5, midtown Manhattan's most prestigious board. Even then, I was protecting our Seventh Avenue turf. I worked with the city on the new zoning, which was designed to protect manufacturing, the same zoning that is now being

replaced because its restrictive clauses left too much unused manufacturing space. During my 25 years on that board, I was the head of new construction in Midtown Manhattan at a time when zoning changes were opening up the heavens to builders who lived by floor-area ratios. Yes, a clothing designer as the head of new construction. I was almost always on the side of the community, questioning height and bulk, trying to get amenities for that extra rental space. When the Museum of Modern Art (MoMA) built its adjoining skyscraper mid-block on 53rd Street and pierced the sky between Fifth and Sixth avenues, the future of the cityscape changed. Every landlord looked to the heavens for their reward. And although I found myself fascinated by the new skyline in our great city, I had trouble with how it was happening. I also ran for chairman of that board and lost by one vote to Joe Rose, a member of one of the city's most famous real estate families. Years later, I actually found out that Susan Rose and her husband, Elihu Rose, were closely related to me. She was my cousin and they were the matriarch and patriarch of the Rose family.

When Donald Trump built his tower on the site of the Bonwit Teller department store, getting permission from the city only if he protected the decorative friezes atop the store and donated them to the Metropolitan Museum. Instead, he pulverized them. He also got extra floors for creating a public space as you enter, the same space now famous for the escalator that announced his run for the presidency. He was supposed to have large enough signage there to entice the public to use the space, and as head of New Construction I called him out for putting a postcard-size sign in a dark corner, instead.

It was time to move on from the community board. That's when I became active in two business improvement districts that I remain on to this day, and why I feel so much a part of the future of the Garment District. As chair of the CFDA, I felt it was a part of my job, and an extension of our design world. In the beginning, I was part of a committee, championed by my good friends, Yeohlee Teng and Nanette Lepore. I also worked with our current CFDA CEO, Steven Kolb, trying to protect enough manufacturing space to keep the word garment relevant for the area.

It's still a work in progress, although at this point as far as I'm concerned, the inevitable is happening. How can one justify sewing a T-shirt in the middle of the most expensive real estate in New York? How does one make sure there is a core and space for showrooms that sell those T-shirts? The clothing racks may be dodging investment bankers, Starbucks replacing Ben's Deli, but we should make sure that working conditions in the area are modernized, revel in the new plazas going up on the avenues, and continue to spritz garmento perfume around the area.

The plaques along Seventh Avenue that commemorate our most prestigious designers are being removed, as too many people are tripping on them. Somehow the plaques that line 41st Street leading to the library, plaques that honor great writers, have not fallen to the same fate. It is now up to the CFDA to decide where they should go

OPPOSITE It was the era of the rolling rack and the egg cream, and I was there and lived it.

where they would not be hazardous. Wherever they go, I have not made it a secret. This garmento wants his own plaque. All of his *schmatta* DNA would consider it an honor to be a permanent fixture in what's left of the Garment Center.

FIRST NAME BASIS

I'm often introduced on QVC by the hosts as a designer who knows everyone in fashion. Not true, but seven decades can produce a healthy portion of famous first name friends. Some of them have become household names. Some I knew long before their metamorphoses; others were already Olympian in stature.

The legendary fashion designer, Anne Klein, was an important part of my young design life. She was a friend and a competitor. We often met at Bill's restaurant on West 40th Street, with its long mahogany bar that all the stagehands at the old Metropolitan Opera House used to belly up to between acts of *Aida*. I called it the Sardi's of Seventh Avenue because if you were anybody, your picture would be on their walls.

Annie and I never met for lunch. It was always drinks, after hours, with her first husband, Ben. It was during one of those evenings that Annie, drink in hand, described her entrance into what was the beginning of sportswear in America. "Parts and pieces, parts and pieces. No woman is the same on top as on the bottom. I'm going to do separates and control my color palate to make it easy for the customer to coordinate her color choices." She told me I should do the same. She did and I didn't, and that wonderful woman is long gone and I'm still here to tell you that story.

We both received the coveted Coty Award in 1969 and co-hosted a big brassy party at the Rainbow Room. It was a boozy night and I found myself on the dance floor with her playing the bullfighter, taunting her with an oversized napkin, flicking it at her and teasing her to follow my lead. She loved it and kept encouraging me to continue until her second husband, Chip, pushed me aside and maneuvered her back to her table. She would constantly tell me to save my favorite styles and keep a record of my work, that people would be interested in years to come. I'm sorry I didn't listen.

She saved everything. Most of it was stored in a warehouse near my hometown of Passaic, New Jersey. A few years after she died, that warehouse burned down and much of her legacy with it. I am so thankful she wasn't around to see those parts and pieces go up in flames, but there was enough DNA to continue, especially when Donna and Louis took over and massaged life back into that extraordinary woman's contribution to fashion.

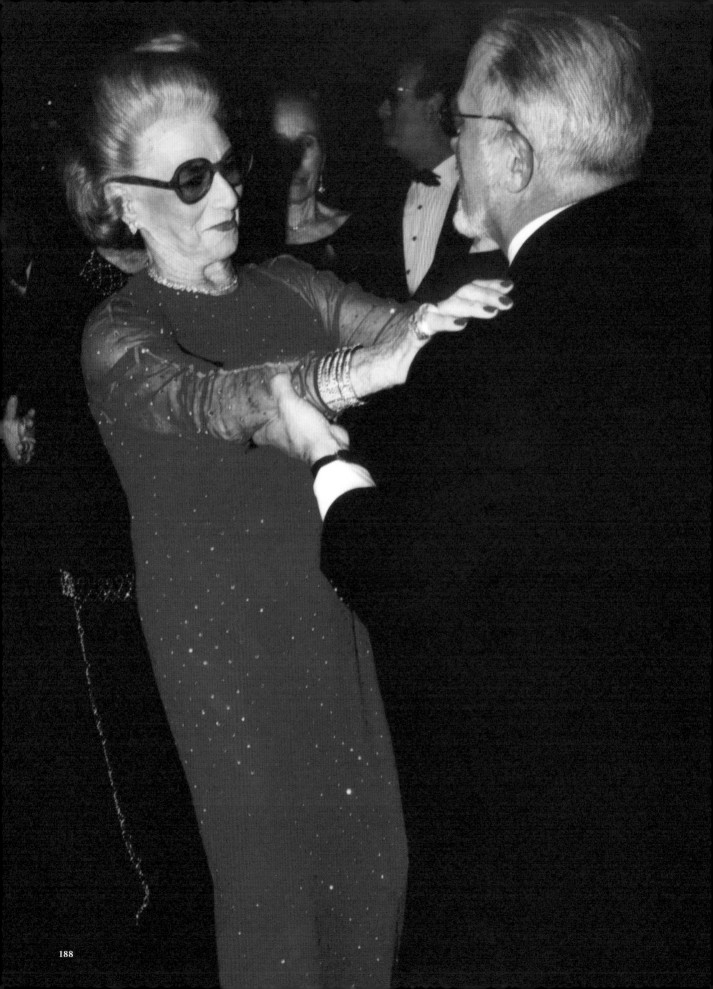

I first met Pauline Trigère in 1955 when I was sent to drop off sketches by Fred Frederics, the less famous partner of John Frederics, of the hat company. His partner, Mr. John, became the superstar at a time when hat companies were considered the height of fashion. Pauline was also very much involved with the city politic, with designers like Mollie Parnis and manufacturers like Jerry Silverman. She was an insider, fraternizing with the power players, namely Mayor Koch and his escort, Bess Meyerson. It was a time when the city was very much involved with Seventh Avenue. There was even a liaison appointed to represent fashion in City Hall. But it was after I was made president of the CFDA that I became, as she described it, her "mensch." P.S. All of her notes to me were written in her signature red ink.

She was my dance partner and my date to many of our galas. She had great gams and was proud of them. One evening, she gave a dinner party at her Park Avenue apartment for a group of designers—Geoffrey Beene, James Galanos, and Donald Brooks. I was starstruck even though I was about their age. They were the galaxy. What really freaked me out was the fact that she had pushed the dining table up against the floor-to-ceiling mirrors and I saw everyone in double. I don't think I ever got over that.

A typical Trigère story was when being interviewed by a newspaper, she kept repeating, I have CRS when she was asked questions. When asked what that meant, she said, "Can't remember shit." She died much too young at the age of 92. I miss the clink of our diamond-cut scotch glasses. The quiet strength of her design, rooted in the European tradition, will never be surpassed.

I met Mr. Blass very early in my career. He was best friends with my first boss, Andrew Woods, and he was one of the first designers I freelanced for, sketching in his showroom, which was then called Maurice Rentner, before it became Bill Blass for Maurice Rentner, and then Bill Blass. I liked Bill. He played the designer part superbly and I also liked the clothes he designed. I was never a part of his flower-filled Grenouille restaurant world but I got to see that world often.

When I became CFDA president, he sat me down in his office to give me the lowdown on the cast of characters on the board. It was that heady list of names that I've already talked about and he had much gossip to dispense. I eagerly listened. It was such a different time then. Many gay designers were still very much in the closet and Bill had a very big closet. I will never forget his telling us how excited he was that anyone on the board that was married could bring his spouse to our gala free.

I had been living with Gene openly for years and when I asked Bill privately what his status would be, he gave me that famous world-weary shrug, and walked away. It's a shame that his design legacy hasn't grown since his death. His licensing deals have melted away and the ladies who lunch have now stopped eating. But when he gave 10

OPPOSITE She had the gams and the graceful step of a ballet dancer— the legendary Pauline Trigère graced our industry with her presence for over half a century. She called me her "mensch." I call her my inspiration.

OPPOSITE 7th On
Sale went West to
San Francisco with
resounding success.
Star power galore
turned out, and I even
got to shake the
hand of Richard Gere
in his prime.

million dollars to the Public Library, it was the beginning of a new era of designers who could afford to contribute to society.

Oleg Cassini was my parrot man. When I first met him, he was married to Gene Tierney and having an affair with Grace Kelly. Who says all designers are gay? I don't remember how I initially got to him, but he hired me to sketch for him. I didn't work at his offices on Seventh Avenue, but reported to his home on East 62nd Street. Every morning, five days a week, his mother, who lived across the street, clocked me in. It was a lonely time. I was the only one in the house. Days were filled with aimless sketching of plunging necklines, perfect for the barstool babies he catered to. I didn't get to see him often. My tenure was short, but I have to say, after I developed my own game of one for Gene and one for Grace, the days went quickly.

Forty years later, after I became president of the CFDA, our lives reconnected. He was an unhappy member who felt underappreciated for his contribution to the fashion world. Truth was, he was never truly accepted by the insiders. Even his contributions to the Jackie Onassis wardrobe were looked down upon by the Givenchy world. I fell in love with his sexy, sly-boots personality and used my influence as the CFDA president to force-feed him a well-deserved award for his contribution. We would often have a casual lunch at his favorite Italian restaurant near his home. Immaculately dressed in blue jeans and blazer—jeans that I presume were custom-made or at least had a designer name stamped on his backside. I constantly asked how I could get a pair. I think it was around Christmas when I received a package with a note, "These are my designer jeans that you love. Wear them well." They were actually Wranglers. I still have them, and they still fit.

When he died, also at the age of 92, he left a complex estate. The world discovered his secret longtime wife who had been running his business with her sister. That business continues to this day. He left me a flock of porcelain parrots that sit on the top of Chinese chimneys to add to my collection. They stand secure on the mantel of the fireplace of my apartment in New York City. Every so often I rearrange them to make sure they don't get bored. I never get bored looking at them and thinking back 60 years to those plunging neckline sketches he probably never saw. One for Gene, one for Grace.

All-out war. There is only one designer in my long and varied career that I didn't get along with, nor he with me. That was Oscar De La Renta. I take nothing away from his contribution. He was a major force and front man for the industry. Many people

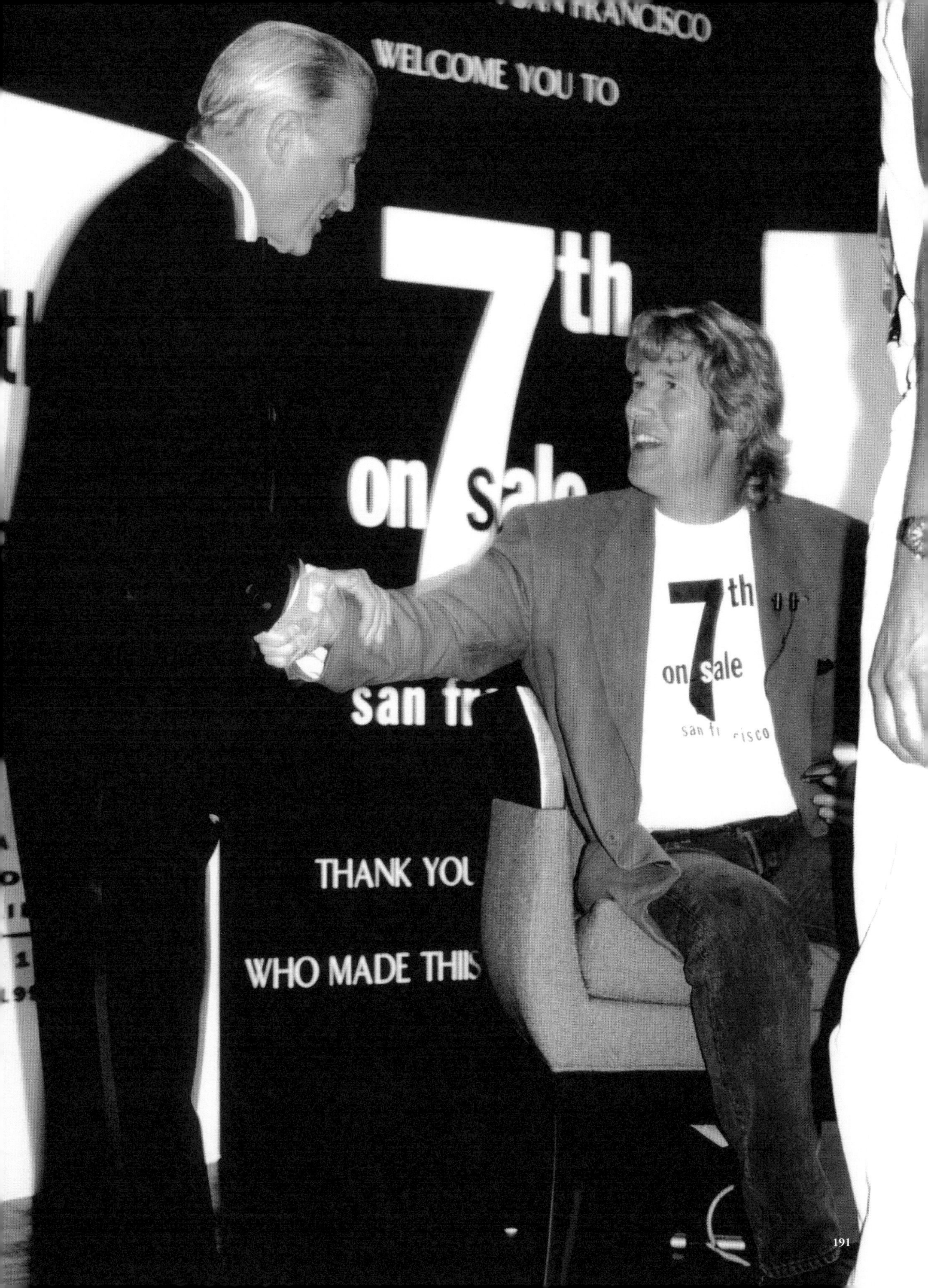
WELCOME YOU TO
7th
on sale
THANK YOU

revere him, especially in his home country of the Dominican Republic. The list of his close friends includes world-class power brokers.

We weren't always enemies. In fact, it was his first wife, Françoise, who discovered my clothes for the revitalized Mr. Mort Company in 1965. Oscar and I even traveled together to Texas to show our collections at the Sakowitz store in Houston. He was then known in the industry as the "cha cha designer." His ruffles announced his entrance. We even got along well while he was president of the council and I was on the board. But once I became president, it was all-out war. As far as he was concerned, I wasn't to the manor born, a phrase that Eleanor Lambert used behind my back. He felt it was his organization and we had different ideas about its mission statement—his more exclusive, mine more inclusive.

In the early years of my presidency, he would call to tell me how it should be done: Often telling me how unhappy Anna Wintour was with me. During that time, our major sponsor was the Hearst Foundation, funded most of our revitalized galas. I was working with Veronica Hearst, Randolph's last wife, who was padding her fashion credentials by aligning the Hearst Corporation with the CFDA. It was during my tenure that I made a trip to Paris to see the fashion shows before we started *7th on Sixth*. It was a big mistake telling Veronica, who immediately took over my itinerary. It was all Concorde class and adjoining suites at The Ritz and I paid for it personally, in more ways than one. Instead of remaining neutral, Patrick McCarthy, my nemesis at *Women's Wear Daily*, cut me dead. Anna, who couldn't have been nicer in the beginning, put on her dark glasses when she realized I was carrying Veronica's train.

On my way home in the Concorde lounge, I watched Oscar sweep in wearing the most beautiful loden coat I had ever seen. This emperor really did have clothes. I sat in the back of that long tube of a plane, sorting out the consequences of having aligned myself with the Hearsts, as opposed to Condé Nast. It wasn't long afterward that I heard it was Oscar who was telling people that I was Veronica's guest. As I've said before, I paid my own way, and somewhere in my messy files, I have the copy of the shocking hotel bill to prove it.

Not long afterward, *7th on Sixth* was born, with Fern's dedication and leadership and the CFDA's backing. The Tents in Bryant Park became a reality. It was on a rainy Saturday, before our official opening, that we invited Ralph, Donna, Calvin, and Oscar for a preview. They were all so supportive and helpful until Oscar arrived, raincoat over his shoulder. After we gave him a run-through, he turned to me and said, "How puny compared to the Parisian venues." Ironic, that over the years, his clothes showed in The Tents longer than anyone else's. But that rainy morning, he certainly rained on my parade, and I never forgave him for it.

I went back to my studio overlooking the tents and festered. Unable to work, I locked up and walked around the corner to 39th Street, right into the porno shop I had passed hundreds of times before. As I looked up the stairs to the Peep Show room,

OPPOSITE Oleg Cassini was once my boss, then a fellow designer, and finally, a close friend. A friendship that lasted until the day he died. I still wear the Wrangler blue jeans he gave me as a Christmas gift, and they still fit.

OVERLEAF Surrounded by fashion royalty: Peter Arnold, who was one of the three executive directors of the CFDA when I was president, and the beauteous Carolina Herrera who could make the simplest white shirt award-worthy.

standing there at the top of the landing was Oscar, raincoat and all. He was juggling a handful of Peep Show coins and, with a flip of his arm, he threw the coins down the stairs and said, "There's only riff raff up here." I said, "Then you should feel comfortable." He walked away up the street. For years, I never told anyone this story except my closest friends. Since he's gone and can't call me, which he would—to tell me it never happened—I feel I can write this now.

Things got so bad between us that when we were both on a flight from New York to Istanbul—just the two of us in First Class—after a perfunctory acknowledgment, we didn't speak to each other for the whole trip. After lots of hors d'oeuvres and much indigestion, I was to be the moderator of a fashion panel and Oscar one of the designers. He came and conquered the Turks and flummoxed me so completely that I took the wrong flight home.

Toward the end of my term, especially after his buddy, Diane, became president and his health deteriorated, we called a truce. Typical of me, I regret that our roles in the council caused a split in our friendship, but I still stand firm about how the CFDA has developed and has continued to grow in the same, more inclusive, direction that was started during my presidency.

✂—

My first memory of Calvin Klein was watching him at the gym on First Avenue, with his spindly legs pushing the bicycle machine. This was long before he could afford his own gym, long before he became the sexy hunk, and very long before his personal life became the country's entertainment. I knew him as a very talented coat and suit designer at 512 Seventh Avenue, known as the Coat Building. Most of the buildings that line Seventh Avenue had their own specialty. The buildings from 498 to 550 were considered the Ivy League of the Garment Center. I vividly remember the moment Calvin decided to widen his design vision and move into sportswear. The company, Lifestyle 70's, that I was freelancing for, thought I should do the same. Once again, Annie Klein, and now, Calvin Klein, found their *fach* but I said, no. I was too busy freelancing after Mr. Mort closed.

Calvin was the perfect example of the designer who had a partner he could trust and respect. It was his childhood buddy, Barry Schwartz. I believe Donna's second husband, Stephan Weiss, was the same for her. And Ralph, well, he had a family support system around him all his life. The pressure of designing is herculean—and how wonderful it can be if there is someone to make sure that it remains your first priority. I will never know if my career could have been a lifestyle brand, but I do believe many of the ingredients were there. I never had the business partner I trusted to make it happen. But this story is about Calvin and I've always wondered how a person feels when he no longer represents his name and that name still represents the person. I should ask him

OPPOSITE The term supermodel could have been invented by the spectacular Lauren Hutton. I've known her since she came north to conquer the fashion world. To this day, she retains "The Look" that is reserved for very few.

one day. A few years ago, as I was fussing over customizing my Range Rover Sport, Calvin just happened to come into the dealership. The color I had chosen was a sneaky shade of beige. Who better than Calvin to ask about that color? With his blessing, I paid the extra $5,000 to have the only Rio Gold Range Rover in America.

It's a well-known fact that movie stars in the 1950s had big heads. The camera loved big heads. Women like Joan Crawford, Lana Turner, Gloria Swanson, Greta Garbo, and Ingrid Bergman, all had big heads. The camera still loves them and one of the more impressive heads today is Diane von Furstenberg. To watch her shake that head and run her hands through its crown of hair is quite intimidating. She can look into your eyes without making contact and completely disarm you with her lyrical Belgian accent. Her glass is always full, and she lets you know when she wants you to drink from it.

She was, for me, the perfect person to become president of the CFDA after my long tenure. I watched her carefully during our board meetings, sitting at the other end of the long table. She always surrounded herself with the stars of the board. Whether it was Ralph or Oscar or Michael. It was my decision to put her on the board after she had rejoined the council. At that point, her meteoric career had lost much of its luster, and she felt like an outsider looking in. But not for long, as her glass was filling quickly. With her marriage to Barry Diller, her sense of confidence seemed to be returning.

Sixteen years is a long presidential tenure, and there were moments when I put out feelers to find my successor. Anna made it known that there was always someone like Calvin Klein waiting in the wings. I believe I even asked Kenneth Cole if he was interested, and how glorious it would be if Ralph were to follow me. Diane was not on that list. And in the last year of my presidency, I was charged by the board to work with them and find my successor. The obvious choice was Joseph Abboud. He had been a loyal member of the board and actively showed an interest in taking on the position.

At the very beginning, he was a board favorite. Most everyone was in Joseph's camp and I, too, felt he had earned my backing, but Diane was not to be denied. Over dinner one evening, she presented her credentials and her vision for the organization. She came prepared and that head of hair stayed in place while she made her case. Over the next few weeks, I did lots of soul searching, waiting to hear Joseph's mission statement. I spoke to almost every board member privately, and the more I probed, the stronger Diane looked. It was probably the few calls that I made to the undecided members that influenced the vote, but I believe it was more the presentations they both gave to the board the day of the election.

Joseph came prepared. In fact, he was overly prepared. His statement was more like a

constitutional directive. He was serious and sincere. He presented first and then left the room. Diane came in without a note in sight, fluffed that halo of hair and charmed almost everyone, but for the few she could never get to vote for her. The secret count wasn't even close. I've never told anyone the final number, but she won decisively.

Her first edict was that there should be term limits of two years. Diane stayed in office for 13. She was the right choice and certainly brought the CFDA to the next level. She felt that she was the "Mother of Us All," constantly using the phrase, "We are a fam-i-ly!" If I were a member of her family, I would ask her for the keys to her pea-green Bentley. (And if she were a good mother, she'd give them to me.)

Probably the boldest name is Ralph Lauren, the designer who looked at a tie and saw his future. He has built a wonderworld of good taste and created a private club that almost everyone wants to be a member of. It wasn't always that way. In the early 1970s, just after Mr. Mort closed, and I had a studio at Henri Bendel, Gerry Stutz asked me if I would take a look at Ralph's new women's line. He too was a Bendel baby, and it was Ralph's first attempt at women's wear. Gerry felt Ralph needed help as he had only been designing menswear before.

His office was on West 55th Street, just above the very trendy Italian Pavilion restaurant. Spiffed up for the occasion, I arrived to be greeted by Ralph, in his blue jeans and white undershirt. His showroom already had the Lauren touch, with more wood per square inch than you find in most forests. When he opened the closets to show me the clothes, they were already a world of controlled elegance—the most beautiful fabrics and tasteful prints in luscious colors, but there was something clunky about them. The placement of darts, the shape and proportions, all lacked the touch of ready-to-wear wisdom he would eventually perfect.

We went downstairs for lunch, he in his undershirt, me in my well-cut blazer. The table was waiting, the food memorable, and the conversation animated. I believe we even talked about the possibility of joint design. I remember how curious he was and how he listened before he spoke, qualities that have served him well all these years.

Many years later, when I was president of the CFDA, and he was on its board, he gave me a ride in his artfully disguised antiquated Cadillac limousine. We were discussing board matters, tooling around the city, he, still in his undershirt and jeans, me, still in my blazer. I was feeling him out about who should be our next president, thinking back to those simpler beginnings, and how far he had come.

He wrote me the most thoughtful note on my 90th birthday, and I still look forward to those Telluride steaks he sends me every Christmas. And, as far as I'm concerned, his placement of darts is now perfect.

OPPOSITE This sketch of DVF came easily, her distinctive posture accurately announces the role she plays]in the fashion world.

Donna Karan pops up in the narrative of my life. I was her guest teacher her second year at Parsons and she manipulated her designing philosophy to the top of the class. She earned my golden thimble award, beating out some of the best students I have ever taught. Her mother ran a showroom next to mine at 530 Seventh Avenue and I can't count how many times she told me how talented her daughter was, and what a big career she was going to have.

I have a picture of Donna and Louis Dell'Olio wrapped in a towel, when posing for a birthday tribute to the actress Dorothy Loudon for *After Dark* magazine. My best technical assistant became her best technical assistant just as she and Louis took over the design reins at Anne Klein. Donna's husband, Stephan, was a Virgo. I believe he was born on my birthday. That is the connection that allows me to watch her from afar with laser-like accuracy.

If I had to choose an American designer that I aspire to emulate, it would have been Rudi Gernreich. He was, for me, the designer's designer, focused and secure to a fault, and clothes that showed a sure hand by their bold simplicity and that remained true throughout his career. You always knew it was a Gernreich.

We bonded briefly when we were guests of the Mikimoto Pearl Company at the Osaka World's Fair of 1969. Six designers were asked to show their collections for two weeks: Count Ferdinando Sarmi, Chester Weinberg, Gayle Kirkpatrick, Victor Joris, Rudi, and myself. We met up with him in Honolulu, as he flew from his home in Los Angeles. Over dinner that night, he gave me the greatest compliment of my design life. He said he'd been following my career and it reminded him of his beginnings. He felt I could inherit his mantle. I melted, and for the remainder of our trip, I was his devoted fan and follower. The only trouble I had was looking into his eyes as his toupee was always askew and I found it hard to focus.

When we landed in Tokyo, everyone was claiming their steamer trunks filled with clothes and accessories for the shows. There were to be two shows per day, and I asked him where his trunks were. He pointed to a small carry-on satchel, and I thought he was kidding. But when he opened it to show me the contents, there were 25 pont de roma knit dresses neatly rolled and folded with matching ballet slippers. The next morning at our model fitting, he chose the exquisite Chinese girls and, as far as I was concerned, stole the show. He already had a reputation in Japan. I believe he was one of the first to license his label in Asia. He told me to do the same, but Mr. Mort closed a year later, and that good advice never happened.

Not too many years later, as his career was winding down, I was asked to take over his

factory in Menomone, Michigan, a shivering cold town on the shores of Lake Michigan. Harmon Knitwear had produced his sublime knit dresses for decades, but the fashion world was turning away from those statuesque shapes and Rudi refused to change with the times. The Harmon family was fast losing their business and was searching for answers. I became that answer and so, for a year, I used their antiquated seven-gauge machines and stilled the circular pont de roma machines. The only store that bought the line in depth was I. Magnin on the West Coast. But it wasn't enough to breathe life back into the business. Those lovely people eventually closed the factory and I have only a duplicate of the original men's thong that Rudi was famous for. I wouldn't dare put it on today. Actually, I gave it to my associate, Michael, years ago. I know he will guard it well.

OPPOSITE I actually own one of the original thong swimsuits that Rudi Gernreich gave me. It no longer divides my backside, and you wouldn't want to see that anyway.

I know he's no longer around to call me at 2 in the morning, especially after not hearing from him for months. He can't tell you his version of his famous name change, but I will. As I've said in this memoir, Arnold was a wunderkind, a smashing success at 22. All kinds of offers filtered into his 53rd Street atelier. One of the big ones was from General Motors, which wanted to use a ball gown of his in a Cadillac ad, but they wouldn't use his name, as it was too Jewish. They had turned down Nettie Rosenstein, and she was a bigger name than he was. So, he seriously started thinking about a name change.

It was at my house in Passaic, over Passover dinner, that we started playing the name change game. Suddenly my Aunt Florence spelled Isaacs backwards and we fumbled with the pronunciation until we settled on Scaasi with an aah. I swear this is what happened, although he eventually described the change in more romantic terms when interviewed. It was my aunt, between the gefilte fish and the matzoh ball soup, that came up with Arnold Scaasi.

He got the advertisement and went on to have a major career for the next half a century. Not an easy man. He could make you crazy with his overbearing antics and late arrivals. His partner, Parker Ladd, was a saint and a perfect foil for his outsize personality. I considered him a lifelong friend and, at his funeral service, I sang the *Shema Yisrael* to him as a payback to the singing lessons he sponsored for me almost 70 years before.

Just last year, when the brilliant Bridget Foley was interviewing me at *Women's Wear Daily*, I talked about Arnold in front of a number of their young staff. Bridget turned to me and politely said that she didn't think they knew who he was. So much for fashion history. Oh, Arnold dear, better that you weren't there. I just heard that you left four million dollars to the Fashion Institute of Technology (FIT). It makes me proud. I think of you often.

OPPOSITE I came dressed as a cowboy and played Cowboys and Indians with my great model Renée Hunter at the Osaka World's Fair in 1969. My short stature felt at home in Japan, but I never truly got into raw fish.

OVERLEAF Like Lieutenant Pinkerton in Puccini's "Madame Butterfly," the beauty of a geisha can seduce you and be life-changing.

And, of course, there was Marc Jacobs. When I opened my studio overlooking Bryant Park in 1975, I created a gracious workspace for the people who worked with me, a duplex with windows that faced north and looked over the tippy top of the London plane trees that, these days, are reaching ancient status and will eventually have to be replaced. Over the years, I've become very friendly with their presence and still marvel at their ability to graciously canopy the frantic activity the park has become known for. Freelance designing was working for me, and between my uniform business, intimate apparel account, and a few attempts to tiptoe back into ready-to-wear, I had a series of assistants who worked for me. They were all full-time and paid for their contributions. I seldom used the apprentice system of hiring people still in school, but if I did hire them, they would be paid. I believe there were many design rooms filled with unpaid talent. It was considered a privilege to work for many. Halston comes to mind. I believe this practice is no longer encouraged.

The apprentices I would take from school came from the High School of Arts and Design on 56th Street and First Avenue. One afternoon, the dean sent five eager students with their portfolios to the studio. I still have the oak table that supported their offerings. One by one, they presented their sketches, and I was ready to move on when the last young boy, with soulful brown eyes, and a confident gesture, flipped open his book of sketches. I still get goose bumps when I think back to that moment. It was all there, the seedling that became the tree known as Marc Jacobs. Of course, I hired him on the spot and alerted Ann Keagy at Parsons to this spectacular talent. He wasn't with me long. He was actually just the young gopher in the studio, but he was already very opinionated about everyone else's contribution and, as I remember, he was working evenings at Charivari, the trendiest store on the west side of Manhattan.

Many, many years later, as I was in the audience, Marc was being interviewed at the 92nd Street Y by Fern in her celebrated series of designer conversations, and she mentioned that I was there, those brown eyes looked out into the audience and said that his memory of those days was how comfortable it was to work in a studio that was so easy and open about one's sexuality. That was most important to him, and it made me blush with pleasure.

If I had to choose one person who represented my ideal Mr. Mort woman, it would have to be Ali McGraw. To this day, when I flip through my meager archive, it's her face and fawn-like stance that seem to best represent my design philosophy. She wore my clothes as if she owned them, and when the person who was dressing her for the movie, *Love Story*, called to ask if they could use my clothes for the movie, I jumped

at the chance. The little pleated dress she wore in the wedding scene still looks modern. These days when we're on the phone, her voice sounds exactly the same, with maybe just a slight drop in pitch. Now in her eighties, facing the Santa Fe sunset, she still exudes honest glamour and good living. I've always felt that she should have gotten a CFDA Icon award. There may still be time. I mentioned it to Tom Ford, our new leader and her Santa Fe neighbor. He seemed genuinely excited by the idea. I'm sure she doesn't care, but I do. We have too few authentic icons in our business that seems to grow them on bushes.

Her voice was in the bass baritone, Wagner range. She would have made a great Wotan, and her talent was as vast as the Ring of the Nibelungen. Liz Claiborne was an early friend of mine. We were together on a trip to the Smithsonian Institute in Washington, DC, coming back from a seminar on emerging young designers. Deep into our scotch slurs, she started on how difficult it was for female designers to get recognition, how all those "homo-sexuals" got the good jobs and all the publicity. She made a good case for it. I told her to get off her ass and make a move with her husband and she did, and the fashion world was hers until it wasn't.

I take no credit for her career, but I like to think that that trip was the seed that started it all. We both moved our businesses into 80 West 40th Street, the same month in 1975. She grew so quickly that she outgrew her three floors. I'm still there 45 years later, looking out at those London plane trees.

HOUSEHOLD NAMES

I may never be a household name in fashion, but I am known in lots of households. That's what happens when you are on QVC for 30 years. I was approached in the early 1990s to face that camera and sell my loungewear. Every showbiz tick started ticking. All of those years when I thought the proscenium arch would be my life now became a possibility. QVC was just five years old at the time and very few designers in my industry took it seriously. In fact, I remember the look of horror on Donald Brooks' face when I told him I was going on the air. For me, it was perfect timing. It all happened when my career was floating sideways and I had not, as yet, become president of the CFDA. In fact, most of the early stars on the Q were flying in the same atmosphere.

My intimate apparel business was enjoying reasonable success until I stumbled onto an end cut of chenille tufted satin in one of the fashion fabric stores elbowing each

other along 40th Street. I had designed a leisure pajama for the Neiman Marcus catalog, and couldn't find where the fabric was produced. A big order and no fabric—a designer's nightmare. It all ended well when I found the manufacturer who produced that very American fabrication in Georgia and Alabama—chenille, the kind you saw in your grandmother's bedspreads and J.C. Penney catalogs, cotton tufted onto sheeting and fluffed to life.

Chenille robes from the 1930s are collectors' items. They caress the body in a manner few fabrics can even pretend to do. They pill and rip easily. No matter; even today, they have avid followers. I still get requests for them, but I haven't used the fabrication for almost two decades. But when I went on QVC, chenille became my calling card, and it was an extraordinary hit. At one point, I sold over a 100,000 wraps in one day and another 100,000 a month later. I even produced chenille teddy bears that became a children's book written by my friend, Kate McMullan, called Nubbies.

I quickly became one of QVC's stars and breakthrough designers. The chenille we think of mostly is knitted and used in sweaters and sportswear. And, for me, it was a natural extension when I joined my friends Beth and Dennis Newman, of the Lizden Company, to extend my reach into the world of knitted chenille. For five years, we were untouchable until QVC began to develop their in-house design teams. There was also more and more competition from those very same designers who wouldn't have been caught dead on the Q years ago.

To this day, I get a kick out of turning on the TV and seeing *The Nanny* schlumping around in my chenille overlay wraps or Estelle Getty, similarly attired, throwing one-liners at the *Golden Girls*. Whenever a stylist needed someone to look Beverly Hillbilly or just out of it, they went to the tufted chenille robes that I was famous for, robes that were made in America until it became cost prohibitive, and off to Pakistan we went. Our machinery in America was tired of tufting. They are still doing it 30 years later, overseas.

But back to QVC, where I had made a whole group of new friends: the host, the buyers, the backstage producers, and my stand-in, Roe Sotorrio. Then, of course, there was Leslie Frank, the woman who 'found' me. There are few hosts who are still facing the camera almost 30 years later: Jane Tracey, Pat DeMentri, Mary Beth Rowe, and Jill Bauer, who just retired. I've had many memorable shows with them. Jane, the cheerleader of all time, can spin a web of seduction like no one else when she stops long enough for the camera to catch up with her. I had an hour show with her in front of a live audience where everything sold out—every sweater, every scarf. There was one sweater she was pre-selling earlier in the show, and it sold out before I even made my entrance. I kissed her and went home. If anything, her motor is even fizzier today.

Pat and her co-host, Dan Hughes, had me as their very first guest in the very first hour of their morning show, and Jill Bauer was my first host and eased me gracefully into the world of television. Then there was the queen of them all, Kathy Levine, who,

OPPOSITE This is one of my Zip Robe Loungers that broke the sound barrier. We sold over 10,000 pieces in one presentation. Eat your heart out, Saks!

OVERLEAF I was Pat DeMentri's first guest on her morning show almost 25 years ago. She still smiles to the camera with that "You can believe me" attitude until this very day. Notice my formal attire.

A-18114
Stan Herman
2- piece
Pajama
Set

RETAIL VALUE
$73.00

QVC PRICE
$49.00

S&H $4.97

Sizes Available
S,M,L
1X,2X,3X

220

-1515   Stan Herman Collection

221

OPPOSITE My Nubby
Stan Bear, wearing
my Nubby Robe,
looking out from my
terrace over the city
I so love. Made of
chenille, my signature
fabric, he has today
become a collectible.

for years, owned the hostess crown, until she didn't. There was the beauteous Scorpio, Lisa Robertson, who tried it on for size and it fit perfectly, for a while. Mary Beth Roe, whose sparkling blue eyes were a mirror into her down-home personality, seemed to capture everyone's love. Caroline Gracie, fellow Virgo, who worked her wonder in her famous closet of goodies. She has kept me in the closet for years. Jayne Brown, who swore she would play tennis with me next time we had the time. I think she's waiting for age to wear me down. And there were the new stars: Sandra, Shawn, Amy, Kirsten, Courtney, Nancy, Alberti, and Jennifer, all of whom have kept me young and somewhat with it. And, of course, all of my Green Room pals, so many that I've shared showbiz chatter with, many who represent the brand, but do not design it.

We all fill the room with eyes on the tote board that tracks the sales. Will it be feast or famine? How many are sold per minute, even second? Will we make goal? All this before the Coronavirus pandemic, when we now work from home. I miss those Green Rooms and, of course, the stable of designers who have become quite impressive: my friends, Bob Mackie, Dennis Basso, Lori Goldstein, Martha Stewart, Isaac Mizrahi, and Susan Graver.

One of my all-time favorites, Joan Rivers, who was also a pioneer before her horrific death, used to yenta with me in her cluttered Green Room. For years, she insisted I was having facelifts. One morning, walking to my dentist's office on 61st Street, I heard that famous voice scream, "I caught ya. I caught ya. You're going to my surgeon." I took her by the hand and led her to my dentist's office that just happened to be in the same building she often visited.

QVC can have almost any designer these days. It's now considered legit to make the big bucks. Just last week, I had lunch with one of our most talented young designers, Jason Wu, who was already immortalized in the Smithsonian Institute with the dresses he designed for Michelle Obama. He was to make his debut in a few months and was truly excited by the prospect.

The other day, I stumbled on a bottle hidden way back in the drawer of my desk. It was the perfume I had created for QVC, appropriately named Chenille. A frosted bottle that contained a few ounces of my much-loved perfume, a shy scent that I believe captured the nostalgia of the chenille personality. It may be the only bottle left anywhere and I intend to keep it until its last spritz.

My life in the intimate apparel world has extended over 50 years, longer than ready-to-wear, even longer than uniforms. The companies, starting way back, are numerous, from Slumber Togs to Carol Hochman, Van Raalte to Kellwood, Crown Tuft to Komar. I've been in almost every catalog invented as the guy that wraps you or zips you into comfort. I've even combined my intimate apparel and uniform worlds by designing robes for the Loews Hotels.

While building the collections, I still sketch in the old-fashioned way and watch the designs come to life without ever touching the fabric. No more work rooms to get lost

in and badger the sample hands. We are off to the Asian rim to make our clothes, and it's shocking how well they're made. This picky Virgo follows the seam line when on camera and plumps up the flare in the hemline while exposing the fabric to a close-up, exclaiming how beautiful it looks.

These days, I've been plumping up the hemlines on AM Style with the beauteous Leah Williams. She just celebrated her 25th anniversary on the Q and continues to charm her way into customers' pocket books. I've always liked my opposite sign. Pisces that she is, she fits the bill perfectly. There is a wonderful blooper that you can pull up if you like that sort of thing. While talking to a woman from south Jersey, who was rhapsodizing about her love for QVC and Leah, someone in the woman's house was interrupting her. Without missing a beat, her voice dropped two octaves and she screamed, "Can't you see I'm on the fucking phone?" Leah rolled with it beautifully, just slightly flustered.

But the story that still resonates with me and sums up my relationship with QVC happened years ago when I was designing the chenille sportswear for Lizden. My most successful piece was a 60-inch wrap with acres of fringe. I produced it in every color imaginable. As I was walking down Fifth Avenue in front of the now-defunct, beloved Lord & Taylor, I spied a woman fashionably wrapped in a chocolate brown version of it. I must have followed her for two blocks when she suddenly turned around and said, "Yes, it's yours. And I'm going for a job interview and if I don't get it, you'll be hearing from me." Where else can you get that kind of response from a devoted customer? It is that connection that has made this medium so satisfying to me. I never did find out if she got that job. I'd like to believe she did.

TAKING THE TRAIN

I almost always drive to QVC. I love driving. I love listening to the opera while I'm driving. I also love the three fried chicken wings I order at Roy Rogers on the turnpike, but there are times when I do have to take the train. Over the 30 years of going to QVC, I've taken the Amtrak Keystone, the sluggish way to get to Harrisburg, with a stop at Paoli, Pennsylvania. I've taken this train often enough to know which side to sit on to avoid the sun. And to complicate matters, the train changes engines in Philadelphia and backward becomes forward. To me, backwards seems nostalgic, while going forward is always fraught with possibilities.

I remember distinctly a particular trip I took. I was seated forward. I had walked east on 34th Street at 8:30 in the morning, most of the glitzy middle market stores still shuttered, yet filled with light and aging merchandise. At Penn Station, I pushed up against a flood of passengers heading to work, coffee in hand. I crisscrossed the

OPPOSITE "King of All He Surveys," a hero one day, and his lackey the next, I've loved my 30 years at the Q, and celebrating this year's anniversary was proof of our mutual admiration.

terminal to get my Dunkin' Donuts coffee, a glazed donut and a bottle of water, and then settled into what is an excuse for a waiting room. New York's Penn Station may be the ugliest, least efficient, major train station in America. It was the stepchild of what was once the grandest train station of them all, stripped and screwed over a half a century ago, left bare-assed for the world to see. It's like a naked man shivering and covering his genitals and asking you to travel with him. Nothing about it is a part of a more civilized order. The waiting room has ceilings that are bathroom height and is painted colors that drain the life from you. I just saw pictures of the new station in the old Moynihan Post Office with acres of glass on its ceiling, a bow to the great Penn Station they destroyed in broad daylight. All this happened just as they replaced the clickety-clack of the departures and arrivals board for an azure blue billboard reminiscent of a fast food chain's menu. I have to admit, for the most part, the trains are on time, and the Keystone plods its way to Paoli with determination.

The Paoli station has a tiny antique coffee shop filled with bric-a-brac and fading train schedules. The proprietor is a woman of substance and manners. Fastidious in her conversation, she can make the simplest action into a complete ballet. I often stop in before the train rushes past her window for a cup of tea. She edges the water to the top in controlled spurts and is always asking how close to the rim she should go, how long she should keep the tea bag immersed and how many cubes of ice to make it drinkable? If I chose a well-wrapped slice of pound cake, she insists on nuking it or otherwise the flavor will not be at its best. We talk of ancient railroad history and her library upbringing slips out in short spurts. She may be a closeted Marxist ready to retire. Paoli will not be the same without her.

My friend, Roe, couldn't pick me up at the station, so Michael arranged for me to be picked up by a local cab company that would take me to QVC, wait there and then get me back in time for the 4:24 to New York. The driver was young, uber-healthy looking, and could have easily posed for the back cover of *Field & Stream*. After a short silence, he asked me where I was from. When I said, New York, he replied, "Oh, from where all those Socialists live?"

These Trumpian days, I'm all set for a fight and this was no different. It became rough stuff before we got to the QVC campus. It reached a crescendo pitch when he accused Hillary Clinton of running a prostitution ring from a pizza parlor in Washington. I had heard that story before, but not in the back seat of a shiny black, spotlessly clean Dodge Durango. There we were, two complete strangers, facing off with no partition to protect us. I could have told him not to wait, but, somehow, I felt the war wasn't over and I asked him to wait for me.

When I told the story to all my pals in the Green Room, they pleaded with me to let him go, but three hours and many dollars later, I got back into his car and, without hesitation, he said that I looked incredible for a 90-year-old man. He had googled me on Facebook and had called his wife, who watched me while I was selling my loungewear

on air. He said he would like to continue our conversation. I asked him to turn around. I wanted to see his face. Without hesitation, I asked if he was a Pisces, and a look of incredulity covered that waterlogged face. I sucked in my breath and asked if he was born on the 12th of March. He was shocked. I looked straight into those confused eyes and said, "I am a homosexual who lived with a man born on that date for 40 years. If only you had half of his love for a fellow man. Why the hell don't you put your gun down and start a conversation with the enemy?"

He did. We talked about his life, his loss of a child and his transient upbringing. He talked more than me, which is an odd turn, and I almost missed my train. Just as I got out of the cab, he handed me his card. I took it and he has become my gun-toting chauffeur of choice. I don't think any of this will make us leave our tribes, but somehow, I feel stronger knowing that my enemy is a human with a heartbeat. I don't even know why I'm writing this story. I guess it's about how two people go bump in the day and find a way to heal. I admit that he was sexy, but that's all I will admit.

What's happening in the world today only makes me feel that these confrontations will happen more often. Better you know your enemy. Better you try to find a small patch of ground to share even if it is barren land. It can be a beginning.

THE PLAYING FIELD

Jan Morris died at the age of 94. As I said at the very beginning, she was the writer who inspired me to sit down once more and write this memoir. Her obituary states that there is one more book to be published after her death. It gives me reason to stay around for a while. My first attempt to write this memoir was 30 years ago, just after Gene died and I had become president of the CFDA. I called the book, *Notes and Sketches*, and it was written as short vignettes. When my agent sent it out to publishers, there was some praise, but no interest in publishing it. I've kept leafing through my life story as friends kept asking me, "Are you still writing? You have so many stories to tell."

Three decades later, I finally sat down in my comfortable burgundy leather chair, the chair that I carried out of B. Altman & Company, the venerable carriage department store, the day they closed for good, and started to write in longhand this journal that is now called *Uncross your Legs*. This time, traveling back to those egg cream days of the 1950s, when our industry was more mom and pop than corporate, with a clearer vision of my role in its makeup.

For those who have never heard of an egg cream, it's a deliriously delicious mixture of chocolate syrup, milk, and seltzer. It's the drink of choice on Seventh Avenue and, if you ask Norma Kamali, it's the exact angle of the glass that accepts the seltzer while

OPPOSITE Saturday morning with Leah Williams has been one of the highlights of my career at QVC. Pisces to my Virgo, exact opposites. We have "wrapped" half the world in Stan Herman.

you're furiously mixing, that makes it perfect and belch-worthy. There is no egg in an egg cream.

I remember the playing field as bush league, a perfect mirror of the times, when the makeup of our work force was flush with middle- and eastern European workers, when my sample hands were almost all Italian and Jewish and the only black faces could be found with a broom in hand. The models, the salesforce, the bosses, the buyers, the press, the sewers, even the mafia, were all very white until they went south for their winter tan.

Seventh Avenue and the dress business, as it was called then, was like show business, always considered liberal and more tolerant, attracting the artsy types who were considered color blind. But much like New York City, home to a rainbow of colors, it was no different than the racism that predominated the rest of the country. I, too, fit the mold of a card-carrying liberal leftist who nodded approvingly at the radical agenda of equality, but lived comfortably, marching only when pushed by the threat of the right.

The first time this threat hit me was in the mid-Sixties when my partners told me I couldn't have a black model in the showroom and Montaldo's, our biggest southern account, wouldn't buy the line. She stayed. They left.

When my elegant French draping assistant refused to fit on the high-assed black model I had fallen in love with, I pushed back. After a heated discussion, she changed her measurements. It was in the late 1960s when the vibrant young Missy Market was the talk of the avenue, that a group of black and brown models began to stake their claim to the playing field. I never did another show without Billy Blair, Alva Chinn, Norma Jean Darden, Beth Ann Hardison, or Renée Hunter on the runway side by side with the white models, Barbara Flood, Tasha Bauer, Jenny Chilcott, and the model I fitted on for over a decade, Bebe Winkler.

Renée came with me to the Osaka World's Fair and opened those Asian eyes with her glowing complexion. Finding black designers was something else. The first one in my life was Willi Smith, a student of mine at Parsons, who left before his senior year. He was never one of Anne Keagy's favorites, the "mistress of fashion," at that very competitive school. She was not known for her love of diversity. My friend, Yeohlee, could attest to that. I believe if Willi had lived longer, he could have been a contender for immortality in the business. He and his sister, Toukie, were two of the first to find the beat of the streets. We did a fashion show together in Dallas for a store whose name I can't remember. The fashion director of that unnamed store gave a dinner party for the designers who were showing there, which included Liz Claiborne.

The fashion director's partner, a hulking stud, got slobbering drunk and started to play the race game about Willi. Before I realized the consequence, I challenged the partner to step outside with me. He was a wuss who melted away when confronted. Willi had already left and when I told him the story the next morning, we shook

OPPOSITE This is my favorite fashion picture of all time. Jeffrey Banks and I—two friends climbing the stairway together, still climbing until this very day, as I finish this memoir.

hands. I turned his palms over and was shocked by the crazy-quilt patterns of his lifelines—deep, dark hand drawings on pale, almost-pink skin. The abrupt ending of his lifelines, which presaged his tragic premature death, still haunt me.

In 1971, the year that I had a studio at Henri Bendel, the star designer of the store was Stephen Burrows, the wunderkind who had stretched his sense of color and fabric with a salad of lettuce edges. I remember him sitting at the machines, his hands manipulating the tension on the fabric, pushing and pulling his way to fame. He was attached at the hip to that store and other than his explosive legendary tableaux at the Versailles fashion show, when he had all of Paris bowing to his sense of style, he never again matched that moment. His clothes today still look modern. He was one of the very first black designers to break through the system.

There were others that followed, designers I knew like Scott Barrie, Fabrice, Byron Lars, Jon Haggins, Gordon Henderson, and, more recently, Eric Gaskins and Patrick Robinson. There was also the explosive talent of Patrick Kelly in Paris. Not a woman in my sightline until Tracy Reese sat around the oak table in my studio asking for advice on her career.

I'm sure there were more, but until the last few decades they all bit around the edges of power and the playing field had a tilted goalpost. Now with the Black Lives Matter movement thundering across the world, exposing the underbelly of racism, I believe there will be no going back. I have had long discussions with one of my closest friends, Jeffrey Banks, the gentleman who has been encouraging me to write this memoir, whom I have always chided for being the whitest black man that I know. I can't believe I have just written that down. He has ridden the roller coaster of fame and failure with the best, having been trained by two of America's seminal designers, Ralph and Calvin. I attribute his longevity to his encyclopedic mind and librarian's sensibility. I also believe he was born with a copy of *Vogue* in his crib. Will his color be an asset in this new order? Will his elder statesman credentials be accepted?

Will I be around to be a part of those changes? Will the shapes and silhouettes of my sketches capture this new ideal? Just a few weeks ago, *Vogue* used my Southampton lake-front property as the setting for their January cover. The world-renowned photographer, Annie Leibowitz, had chosen the location and came armed with her dedicated crew to photograph the newest sensation, Paloma Elsesser, emerging Rusalka-like from the lake, a woman of color with curves that would enhance an Alpine mountain pass and a canvas of facial features that made love to the probing lens of Annie's camera. This couldn't have happened, even a decade ago. Over drinks that evening with Paloma, I thought back to the years when even thinking of fitting on a black model was considered radical, revolutionary, revolting, and when the Mason-Dixon line between stockroom and showroom was impenetrable. The playing field is finally in flux; the tilt of the seesaw is leveling off. There is still so much work to be done. I feel privileged as an elder statesman to have a ticket to the game.

THE PARTY IS OVER

It wasn't more than a few weeks after Diane was anointed president of the CFDA that the doors slammed shut. Sixteen years is a long time to head an organization with the power and the potential of the CFDA. But, once over, your status is now history.
Under the leadership of Anna Wintour, the *Vogue* CFDA fund gave its first gala party. I was seated so close to the toilets that the noise of their flushing drowned out the background buzz around me. I was suddenly irrelevant, 16 years wiped away without a mention of my name during the evening. I was pissed that my term as president went apparently unrecognized.

The moment the program was over, I whisked out my fan and waved down a cab, figuring out what I would say to Diane. Before I got home, my cell phone rang and it was her, apologizing. Would I ever forgive her? I guess I did, but the wound is still there. She has now given 13 years of her golden time to the council and Tom Ford held that position, and now, Thom Browne. I doubt that Diane will ever be seated next to the toilets, but who knows?

In all of the years I was president, I asked Diane to walk the red carpet with me a few times, but she would always say something like, "Oh, Barry gets jealous when he sees me with another man." Did she actually believe I believed her? It's different today. I am no longer irrelevant. She tends to look me straight in the eye. In fact, often when I'm with her, she asks when was the last time I had sex. When I tell her it was just that morning, she fluffs her hair and says, "Oh, I gave that up years ago."

In the beginning, Diane only wanted a two-year term; she even wanted the bylaws changed so there would be limitations to the presidency. She found out how quickly two years go by, and those two became 13. She brought immense power to the organization. Her connections are legendary, and she really worked at the job. Steven Kolb was the perfect executive director for her, new to our business, bringing no baggage with him when he took the job. When we hired him, I used to make fun of his square-toed shoes. He has since become more fashionable and wears sneakers and shrunken suits. As I write this, he is now adjusting to Mr. Ford's power base and leadership. Up until the arrival of the Zoom world, Diane sat across from me watching the newcomers jockeying for power. The pandemic has now given new shape to the table. Everyone sits in their own universe, surrounded by the comforts of home, available waist up, no one to rub up against or to feel their body language and marvel at their forever-young personalities.

The other woman who walked beside me all of those years, keeping her distance with a frozen smile, was Eleanor Lambert. There was a moment in time when she invited a group of designers to go with her to Oklahoma. She was well connected with the government process and her famous show in Versailles was a perfect example of her

power base. The reason for the junket was to use the Native American workforce as a factory for American fashion. Apparently, Oklahoma was a state that 15 tribes were pushed into, and unemployment there was over 50 percent. I think I was the only designer who almost produced results there. I had one of the tribes make native fabrics for my licensed bag line, incredible indigenous weavings that I sold to two major department store chains. There was a written contract, with the sample fabric priced at $5 a yard. When it came time to order stock, they were asking $25. I lost my orders and my bag licensing and my desire to ever go back to Oklahoma.

Eleanor died at the age of 100, having attained legendary status. During the last years of her life, she was still trying to take back the council. She felt it was her baby. I was told that there were even lawyers working on it. I can understand how Eleanor felt. Even after 18 years since leaving the presidency, I find myself still involved. While sitting at board meetings, I think back to those heady days and how quickly the council became the catalyst for a sleepy industry, the way it responded to the global thrusts of fashion, and the warmth and camaraderie generated by a motivated membership. So many new friends and so proud to feel a part of fashion's future. That party may be over, but for me it's not yet time *to call it a day*.

OPPOSITE Body language says it all and there's not even an argument that she's the most influential voice in fashion in the last quarter century. There may never be anyone like Anna Wintour again.

OVERLEAF If you look carefully, you can see me lying in the hammock watching Gene looking into the camera for posterity. Two of us on the point of land I still call Paradise.

PART IV: A FULL LIFE

When I look back at the arc of my life, I have few regrets.
The early death of Gene is the bold exception.

THE PARLOR CAR

When people find out how long I have been in the Hamptons—at this moment it is 64 years—the first thing they ask is, "What was it like then? You must have seen lots of changes." I did. Although I still feel the East End of Long Island is special and I will be there until I die, it's not the same. Those potato fields and untouched dunes, the empty back roads, and the shuttered estates are long gone. But what I miss most are the Pullman parlor cars that made up the Cannonball Express, the 4:30 pm out of Penn Station. Aging, plush swivel chairs lining either side of the car, far enough from each other to ensure privacy. If my memory is correct, I think there were Persian runners the length of the car and there was a bar car to start the weekend the minute you got on the train. They were old Pullman cars, hand-me-downs from the railroad's heyday. There were even a few compartment cars that gave you the feeling you were on a tacky Orient Express.

For me, those trips every weekend during the summer months, 100 miles of track from city to beach, represent the Hamptons I knew in the 1950s. Just the way the countryside changed as the train moved eastward. The sudden sight of duck farms in Moriches. A quick glimpse of water when Quogue appeared. All those families waiting for the breadwinners who arrived for the weekend. For me, it was Gene waiting at the Southampton stop, always in the same spot, competing with Charlotte Ford screaming for Edsel, Mayor Lindsay waving down his distracted Mary, and Cathy di Montezemolo, the *Vogue* editor and fashion icon, picking up her bike for the trek to the compound.

My first trips with Gene were by car, almost five hours from the city, four on a good day. That is why the Hamptons were exclusive, and the fact that it was a resort without hotels. Day tripping was adventurous and the season was short—the end of June to September. Few people stayed later, although, as I remember, there was a small group who remained until the holidays, celebrating Oktoberfest before leaving for Florida. There were also lots of locals who felt privileged to mingle with society, who serviced their homes and country clubs. It was very Republican and very white. The biggest tension was between the Catholics and the Protestants. The Murray family compound with its imposing high wall was the Catholic foothold in Southampton. There wasn't a Jew in sight, but they were there. The cemetery in Sag Harbor is proof of that.

In Southampton, the few that were known were the merchants: the Goulds, the Presses, Shep Miller, and the Silvers. Those are the ones I knew. The woman, Revel Biggs, who sold me the property I live on, had married into one of the upstanding local families. Her lover, Bill Dunwell, was the town historian and ran the Southampton Beach Club. She loved rubbing up against the privileged class and took on many of their attributes. She was also considered by many to have witchlike powers and played that part well at the Historical Society summer parties. She was the first person who read my horoscope, beginning a lifetime interest in astrology. She became Gene's and my surrogate mother. I'm still living on the property I bought from her, and as I look across the lake, the vista is the same, only the trees are taller and a few more houses are clinging to the shoreline. The movement of the seagulls, mallards, and Canadian geese still ruffle the waters, cleansing their feathers. In fact, not enough has changed to drive me away from this paradise. Just a walk on the beach in the winter's sun can revitalize these bones.

I have watched the village of Southampton closely over these years. Downtown, Jobs Lane, once considered one of America's great shopping resort streets, can no longer compete for that title. The silhouettes are the same, but the shuffle of the storeowners has changed. Rents have skyrocketed and few can stay in an all-year 'round business. There are a few landmark stores left like Herbert & Rist, my liquor store, rubbing up against a Carvel, antique stores that no longer have the panache of Caldwell Alexander's seminal store, and many, too many, women's boutique clothing stores filling the spaces that used to sell groceries.

Although we've lost Bob Kean's historical bookstore and Southampton's first art gallery, we still have the country's oldest department store, Hildreth's, and I have the second-oldest charge account there. Herrick's Hardware still has its squawking parrot greeting you when you enter the back way, and the great Catena family still dispenses the best meat in town and remains a Democratic oasis in this Republican stronghold. Of course, there's Shippy's Pumpernickel, still sizzling steaks, one of which almost killed me before my cousin Lloyd applied the Heimlich maneuver. John Duck's, long gone, was Friday night dining for almost everyone. The great chef, Craig Claiborne, used to sleep off his hangover in the parking lot in the only other Rover sedan on the east coast and I so often had to wake him up to tell him he was in my car.

Just the other day, Silver's, the last soda fountain-turned-restaurant, closed forever. The Goulds, the Millers, and the Press family are long gone. We have our Ralph Lauren and we used to have Saks Fifth Avenue, but Southampton has never become the boutique for the wannabes. East Hampton easily takes that prize.

Now that I am in my sixth decade in a house that I shared with Gene for almost 40 of those years, the choice to move here was a wise one. It could have been Connecticut, the Catskills, or the Hudson Valley, but it was this lake that lured us. The Hamptons today seem so posh and untouchable to so many people, but to the two of us, it was always home, even if our new friends were sometimes famous names and we squeezed the same vegetables at Schmidt's that the power players did. We treated it the same way anyone treats their hometown. I get my mail, shop for food, fill my car with gas, call the plumber to fix the toilet, see my brother's family for Friday night dinner, have my car washed every two weeks, get my 20-pound bag of bird feed with a hand gesture

at Lynch's, now Fowler's, and complain about the traffic and those new people sucking up the air.

Oh, yes, it has changed in almost 70 years, but I can live with those changes. Just walking on the beach, either on the bay or the ocean, brings everything into perspective. By the way, the trains that come out from the city these days are no faster than those parlor car days, but you can be sure there is not a swivel chair in sight.

THE COMPOUND

It sounds so positive, so inviting, just calling it *the compound*, makes this slim peninsula on the shores of Big Fresh Pond and, if you speak Native American, Lake Missapoge, a glorious place to live. I've been on this sliver of sand in the North Sea section of Southampton for over 60 years.

It all started in 1955, the year Gene and I locked into what would become our 40-year relationship. These days, I would have called it a marriage. I had seen the property the year before, the year that we separated, when Gene felt, and rightfully so, that I wasn't ready for a commitment. This hussy was already having an affair with the handsome Louis Thayer, son of the upstanding hardware store owner in Bridgehampton. Thayer's Hardware still sits proudly on the runway they call Main Street, crushed by all of the real estate offices selling property in the much-beleaguered potato fields on the East End. Lou and I had driven to Southampton to visit with my head tailor, Joe Saia, from the Martini Company that I was picking up pins for. Joe's boss, Sylvan Rich, and his lover, Jerry Silverman, had rented a little cottage on that same lake, and with Sylvan's wife, Ellie, the threesome were swimming and sunning far from the famous estate section we think of as the Hamptons.

One look and I knew I would be back. When Gene and I found our way into each other's lives again, one of the first things I did was to drive him out to see what I had fallen for a year earlier. I vividly remember our drive down to the compound from North Sea Road. The first person we saw was Revel Biggs, a woman who became our surrogate mother, roasting weenies over what was to be the most constant fireplace in our lives.

The compound had two houses: the Green Camp and the red-shuttered cottage. It was the cottage that Gene and I had rented after convincing Revel that, instead of renting for two weeks, we would stay for the whole summer. I watched Revel and Gene feel each other out, relax and fall in love over the well-done weenies. It was a surprising marriage: she, a conservative Suffolk County Republican who moonlighted as the town's backstreet witch, and Gene, an authentic liberal with a revolutionary underbelly. That love lasted until his tragic death almost 40 years later.

OPPOSITE My surrogate mother, Revel Biggs, town backstreet witch, and upstanding Republican East End citizen. She filled our lives with her bigger-than-life personality. It is her property that I now live on, and everywhere I look she is present.

OVERLEAF This is my very first sketch of our hot-waterless shack on the lake's edge. This is where we spent 15 summers before it faced the wrecking ball and became just mere memories.

PAGES 248–249 Revel Biggs and her boys on what she called the campus in the 1940s. The cabin was used as a bunkhouse for her husband's Ridgefield Park, New Jersey, football team. Notice the spruce trees that are now 80 feet tall and the fireplace that still comforts me with the wood my friend and neighbor Grant Greenberg burns for our weekly cookout meals. He can even fry the perfect sunny-side-up egg on its flickering flame.

249

The point, as we called it, was all her property, which included a third house on a bluff closer to the road. I bought that house before she died, and the compound was complete, and has made my busy life in New York possible.

In the beginning, it was five nights in New York, then four, then three, and recently, during the pandemic, an occasional one. The Green Camp is a wonderful camouflage green, giving it its name. The structure was a store on Main Street before it was brought up from the village the year I was born and, except for an added-on bedroom, it is exactly as it was in 1928. It has been home to some notables over the years—my bosses, Gerry and Sylvan, two of Seventh Avenue's movers and shakers of the time; to the great choreographer, Jerry Robbins; and to the painter, Wilhelm de Kooning and his mistress, Ruth Kligman. I have rented it to a series of architects and landscape architects. In 1991, the very first year I met Fern, the year Gene died, she rented it for a decade before I convinced her to buy her own house down the road with a magical view to the west. My longest tenants were the Barrow sisters, both Simon & Schuster publishing production experts. In fact, even today their names come up in conversations about publishing.

The red-shuttered cottage that I had to knock down to build a house with hot water and a john you could enter from the inside, was home to Revel's husband's football team from Richfield Park, New Jersey. The house came down in 1969, and other than the fading pictures taken in those early years, little of it remains. It stands tall in a painting I did the day before the wreckers came to plow it under. Fifty years later, there are still small shards of window glass clinging to the shoreline, constant reminders of those good old days.

When we finally built our house, Bill Dunwell, Revel's lover, insisted on clearing the point to expose a sandy beach that has seen many naked torsos skootch into the lake. Revel and her best friend, Nina Olds, Gore Vidal's mother, would often take their martinis and face the sun, topless, on the point. Our new house was brought down in pieces from Massachusetts. I found the house on the roof of the Abercrombie & Fitch store on 57th Street. It was being shown as the newest way to build a house in parts and pieces. I felt confident enough to skip the architectural exercise and, within a month, this jewel of a house was facing the elements and enjoying their company.

It has aged well. The cedar inside has developed a satiny patina and the constant flow against the windows makes you feel part of nature. The three fireplaces catch the flames quickly and give the brick facade that feeling of efficiency and luxury in its simple surroundings. And those fires have seen many sunsets and snowstorms, heard much Wagner and Schubert, and watched as we made love as the stockpot bubbled.

When EEGO was formed, many of the initial meetings were held at the house, and Gene led many conscious-raising meetings during the AIDS epidemic. It was, and still is, a perfect place for parties as long as the weather cooperates, with a long groaning table facing the dock, and space for people to wander to the point that faces northeast.

In the beginning, we used our sunfish to race our neighbors in the Labor Day regatta, seldom catching the wind when needed. There are still three canoes and a kayak to yenta along the shoreline. There used to be an abundance of blueberries, but the birds from the sanctuary usually got to them before we did.

I was president of the Lake Association for over 20 years, which meant we would often meet in our house. I'm still a member, but have been much less active, watching the newcomers ask the same environmental questions we asked 40 years ago. The lake is clean, clear, and except for the lily pads taking too much oxygen from the sandy bottom, has the distinction of being the poster child for Long Island lakes. To swim in it is to love it. When we first moved there, we actually took baths in its soothing waters, but that stopped as soon as we realized the adverse consequences on the environment.

The snapping turtles still pop up, surveying the shoreline, daring us to swim. They are actually harmless, but they play their role well as keepers of the lake. Once a year, a few will hobble onto the point, lay their eggs, and move on. We have big mouth bass and a few perch that are natural and not stocked by the state. Fishermen sport fish all year long, even cutting into the winter ice—less since global warming, but they throw the catch back to live another day. Every spring, the Alewives wriggle in from the North Sea Harbor, jumping the manmade drainage dam to spawn and start their life cycle. There is a finite amount of land on the shoreline since we saved a third of the lake as a bird sanctuary. Many of the old-timers have passed on, but the new people seem very environmentally savvy, so I feel good about our future.

Just last month, the two gentlemen I sold the house on the bluff to and to whom I now rent the camouflage Green Camp, got married. It was a simple, elegant ceremony for just eight people. They asked me to say something, and I jumped at the chance: *It was 65 years ago that I stood on this very spot in the embrace of the man I would live with for almost 40 years. How proud he would have been to see this wedding today, to watch the wonder of these two men, Ivan Bart and Grant Greenberg, exchanging vows, vows that were denied to us until my good friend, Edie Windsor, who spent much time on this dock, changed the rules of the game with the Supreme Court ruling on gay marriage. How pleased and shocked he would have been to see the Mayor of Southampton officiating. It's moments like this that make all the difficulties we face seem manageable, even conquerable.* There will be many more treasurable moments on this dock. This compound will brighten lives long after I am gone. Someone may suddenly see a glint in the sand coming from glass left over from that wrecking ball. They may not know its origin, but just being there, they have become a part of this lake's legend.

OVERLEAF The day before the wrecking ball came to crush our love nest shack, I stood 10 feet out in the lake and painted this picture in one day. My nervous strokes seemed to have captured the fragility of its charm. And, as it should, it now dominates the living room, sitting comfortably on the patinated walls of cedar, sheltering over 150 bird figurines I've scattered in every corner.

PAGES 254–255 Books bending to the passing of time. 78 rpm records long unplayed, the wall that constantly reminds me of the past, and is watching me face the future with confidence.

patricia underwood
PERRY ELLIS
THE GOLDEN RETRIEVER
PHOTOGRAPHIC SOCIETY
BRUCE WEBER
TASCHEN

255

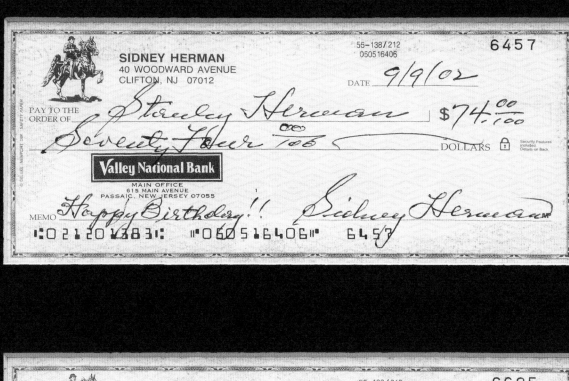

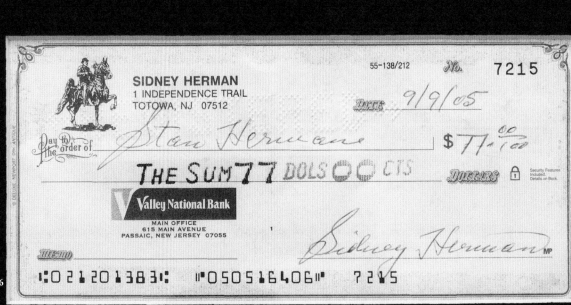

STUFF

It takes a lot of stuff to fill 90 years of living. From the moment you're born, stuff begins to accumulate. In the beginning, everything needs to be functional—your first diaper, your first crib, gifts to start your life in comfort, purchases that probably affect your choices the rest of your life. I've always wondered how soon one's taste level sets in. I certainly have thought about that since my chosen profession exposes my choices every time I put pen to paper.

I realize how consistent the stuff I have purchased all these years has been. My choice of color, texture, and silhouette remains the same, whether it's a sofa or an SUV, suits or sheets. I can draw a connection all the way back to my childhood, rejecting a collarless blazer my father purchased for me and wincing over the *tchotchkes* my stepmother polished every night when we were asleep. I am now surrounded by all my choices. They've been piling up and adding to the neat clutter in my studio, apartment, house, and life.

Stuff, books, records. Yes, I still have 78 rpm records holding up the wall in my country home, oak tables that looked aged when I bought them 60 years ago. My apartment holds a museum of well-framed photos, and framed travel drawings follow you up the staircase to my bedroom. There are unused dog bowls long after Mo died, iron skillets that have always competed with my Le Creuset cookware, dinnerware so heavy you could collapse under the weight while setting the table. I've kept the thread of my purchases, unraveling from the same spool. I've had the same house and the same apartment for over 50 years, the same studio for almost as many. And the stuff I've chosen to fill those spaces still comforts me.

Consistently, I've never covered my windows with curtains. Even in New York where your next-door neighbor could tell you that you need a manicure. I keep my blinds up. The studio has 12-foot windows overlooking Bryant Park, not a curtain in sight. And my lake house has uninterrupted sex with nature, all four seasons.

The colors I've always lived with are from the earth. They usually have a well-aged personality. No red, but deep burgundy. No royal, always navy and green. The color of nature is always in my house with all my living plants, plants that seem to love me as they stick around forever. I have one pot sitting on the fireplace mantel whose shoots have traveled up the brick facade for 40 years. The soil continues to pump life into its leaves as they look down on my sun-bleached furniture.

The rooms of my life are full. There is no place for a major purchase unless I am replacing an older one. The only changes have been electronic television sets that are designed for obsolescence. They have completely pixilated my existence. The closets are full. The weight of wool has bent every bar attempting to hold them. Some of my early purchases have reached antique status: My first six-button Yves Saint Laurent

OPPOSITE I stopped cashing my birthday checks when I hit 70—checks that my father wrote in his impeccable script, a dollar for every year I had lived. He complained that his checkbook never balanced, but the idea of framing them for posterity pleased him. There was always a sense of order to his life.

blazer and probably the only Geoffrey Beene unconstructed corduroy jacket in existence. Ornery as he could be, not a pocket to put your hands in. There are the Armani suits catching dust in their deep-pleated pants and oversized slouch, Donna Karan's sleek cashmere attempts at making her mark in menswear, and even the tuxedo she made for me when I first became president of the CFDA. It's disgusting that I haven't called Housing Works to give my things all a new life with someone who needs them.

It's a good thing I've started collecting birds. They are small and seem comfortable in their settings. My house has almost 150 of them perched everywhere, looking out at the mallards on my beach, birds I feed twice a day when I'm home. That and all the window bird feeders in my sunroom—feeders that keep me content, watching the push and pull of the squirrels, vying with the woodpeckers and cardinals.

Virgos are supposed to be neat. I broke that assumption years ago. My house looks neat, but my closets are a shambles. Only I know where the toilet paper is. My dear friend, Victor Bonfilio, comes all the way from San Francisco every year to stay with me. In one week, he organizes everything: My CD collection alphabetized, Janet Baker next to Berlioz, Richard Strauss next to Smetina. He even culls out my collection of books, most of which were purchased when Gene was alive.

Stuff. Cans of salmon hiding on the top shelf, spices that have long lost their kick, platters that go as far back as my Grandma Tannenbaum. Rugs that left their native lands before the turn of the last century. The 12-foot rubber tree that I lost during the pandemic that has sheltered me for over a half century. There is no more room for pictures or paintings. No more shelf space for dishes or glasses. No hooks left for the pots and pans lining my brick fireplace in the kitchen, a kitchen that has a history of rich stews and stockpots. The butcher block drawers are littered with every imaginable kitchen utensil. And every time we cook communally someone says, "Fern, where's the lemon squeezer?"

The wooden floors are slightly warped from all of the neighbor's dogs shaking themselves down when they get out of the lake and my good-natured housekeepers, Kathy in the country, as well as Rosa in New York, move things just enough to keep the disorganized order I love in place.

I know it's a bit of a stretch, but I put cars in that 'stuff' category. There are three boys in our family. My brothers, Harvey and Mitchell, are car buffs, and I guess I, too, can be included in that category. Harvey collects cars, mostly European, but he lost his heart to a 1968 Chevy convertible and there was no going back.

My brother Mitchell is more muscle. He gets his rocks off from American cars of the last century. He can polish a fin with his cashmere rags until his reflection takes over the room. He never takes his favorite car out when it's raining. Harvey purchased a 1949 red Chevy truck just yesterday. He will tool around Hampton Bays until he gets bored and moves on. But I love watching his 89-year-old eyes sparkling behind the wheel.

OPPOSITE The fireplace built lovingly by the artisan who fell in love with this house, a fireplace constructed with bricks he salvaged from the estate section. It now supports the oldest plant in the room that sprouted from a single pot that has lasted 40 years. Its searching leaves seem to caress the barracuda that has been swimming south while watching over my comings and goings in this glorious setting.

And I love cars the way I love fashion—all shapes and silhouettes, all textures and colors. Like everything else in my life, I have been consistent. Back in the 1960s, I purchased my first car. Until that point, Gene had been the purchaser. Steady income as a teacher was bank-creditworthy so the two Corvairs and the French Renault were his choices. I still love those motors in the back Corvairs that Ralph Nader put to bed for their accident-prone record. There is one sitting in the fields out here completely rusted out, sprouting flowers and looking like a giant vase. Our second Corvair ended up with my brother Mitchell, who put his foot through the floor the first time he drove it.

I gave my heart to the British Rover Corporation, the same one that makes the iconic Defender. I bought a Rover 2000TC in 1969 and had it customized in London with a sliding leather roof and air conditioning. They didn't use air conditioning in European cars then, maybe not just in Rovers, but they plopped that unit on top of the engine and every time I had to fix the car, which was often, they had to remove the air conditioner before they could work on it. I kept that car for 25 years. Its electrical system wouldn't run a flashlight, but it was mine and it was special and nobody else wanted it, except for the food critic, Craig Claiborne. One afternoon, when Gene was picking me up at the Southampton train station, I spied Ralph Lauren eyeing its sexy lines. He's always had great taste. When the Rover finally died, I gave it to the gentleman who worked on it all those years. He professed great love for it. Two weeks later, I watched it flat-bedded to the junkyard, only the outer shell intact. I never spoke to that guy again.

We had a little red Volkswagen convertible that Gene looked great in. It was the silliest purchase we ever made. We drove that car from city to town with our giant poodle Mo skootched into the space behind the back seat. After Gene died, I gave the car to his niece, Shana. Within two weeks, she had totaled it. It was a slippery night and she was devastated.

The car that I always wanted was the Land Rover Defender, but Gene hated shift cars and I fucked him up with an ornery stick shift Jeep back in the 1970s. I wouldn't do that again. Just after he died, I decided the next best thing was the new Range Rover, the car that started the trend of expensive SUVs, a car that could take you to the Belham Castle front door as well as its off-road back doors. I fell in love with it long before it was legal to bring them into the United States. My first was in 1991, and I've had at least six versions of it since, long before the yuppies discovered its secrets.

Here in the Hamptons, it's as popular as Toyotas. The last few have been the Sport version. Mine was a souped-up V8 that has a burble that Lamborghini would envy. Just last month, after waiting almost 30 years, I ordered the new Defender. It will be making the journey from Solihull this October and the circle will be connected. It's a shy, sandy green with a white roof and all its macho finishings. I think it looks like an ice cream truck. I may get a bell instead of a horn and become the Good Humor man.

All this stuff. Last year I started to list it. My will should make some sense of it all. Who will get the Jim Dine painting and the Jane Freilicher pastel? Who might still listen to classical CDs? Who would want all those sketches on the staircase in my apartment or the plants that I've watered all these years? Like everything I do, there is no order to my order, and unless I keel over from a sudden heart attack, I figure I can still find a place for all this stuff.

SOUTHAMPTON SAND

I've walked the Hampton beaches for over 60 years, the last 30, alone. No longer watching the fading silhouette of Mo's black body in the distance, no longer arm in arm with Gene into the brilliant sunsets, no longer cruising the dunes for a quick encounter with the horny locals. So many years, so many friends, so much history.

The East End shoreline is a long stretch of beach, miles of sand creeping up the shifting dunes that act as barrier for the ocean's constant pounding. Every few miles there is a public access and each access has a name. The two that I've entered these past 60 years are called Flying Point and Fowler's.

In the beginning, before there were lifeguards and PortoSans, the beach to go to was Flying Point. It was the Southampton art colony's choice and because of its nurturing nature, home to a large contingency of gays. Some very famous names, some city dwellers, some sun-and-sand worshippers. The beach game of choice was Scrabble and I found myself avoiding this very competitive exercise that Gene reveled in. I knew my limitations. I very often joined Jerry Robbins' group, sheltered in the dunes so you could sunbathe nude.

The leader of the Scrabble pack was a dedicated kaftan dresser, Lee Kressel. His battery of bitchery could sink an armada. At this point in his life, he was the go-to director for dubbing movies from Italian to English. He was working directly with Federico Fellini and they had taken on many of his cutting Italian directors' mannerisms. He usually won at Scrabble, although another friend, Stanley Posthorn, often gave him a run for the title.

The very young, very blonde, and very beautiful Terrence McNally, and his entourage, which included his current lover, Bobby Drivas, had the biggest blanket. The painters, Jane Freilicher and her husband, Joe Hazan, who lived within walking distance from the beach, were often entertaining the poets John Ashbury and Kenneth Koch, in clusters with John Gruen and his beautiful painter wife, Jane Wilson. Actually, Jane started her life in New York as a model on Seventh Avenue.

The dual pianists, Arthur Gold and Robert Fizdale, with their guests would often share blankets fully dressed. It was a beach with no pretense, just regulars, long before the *anschluss* of matched sportswear and attitude began to vie for space. It was when these newcomers discovered this stretch of sand that we all moved westward to the next cut, Fowler's, named after the gentleman who owned most of the land that surrounded its pristine beach. Lots of unmonitored parking, no lifeguards, and even higher dunes that held their grass without fear of encroaching on the mega mansions that were beginning to dot the landscape.

It was the gay world that was reeling from the AIDS epidemic that came to that beach to cry in private while sunning and cruising that made this public beach famous, too famous for the town officials in Southampton. Suddenly, parking was drastically limited, access almost completely cut off. In the beginning, there was frustration, but no response, until the newly formed gay group called EEGO, the acronym for East End Gay Organization, and a few well-connected friends, walked to the town hall and confronted the town's supervisors, forcing the Fowler's to reopen right away. It was more complicated than we expected, but in the end, we got our precious parking back and solidified our presence in Mr. Fowler's backyard.

Until today, if you walk to the left, you're confronted with buff male bodies, a volleyball net, and elegant table settings. To the right, the blankets are set with healthy lunch pickings for the burgeoning lesbian population. The straights, often bombarded when they see the scene, leave the middle muddled and end up on the very western edge.

There are so many pictures in my photo albums, most reminding me of walks on Fowler's beach. These days I walk the beach with my friend, David, watching his lovely lab chase the gulls from sand to sea, nodding at the silhouettes of passing strangers.

I remember years ago when I was designing the uniforms for McDonald's and they asked me where I wanted to test them. One of the places I chose was Riverhead. Actually, it was one of the few fast-food chains at the end of the island. We started our mission in Tucson, flew back to Chicago and onto Riverhead. I was sitting with the pilot in the private jet as we circled over the skyline in New York and eventually cut engines a few miles from the Westhampton airport. Suddenly concrete turned to green, and miles and miles of sand touched the great Atlantic shoreline. The pilot turned to me and questioned where we were. He thought we might be over the Cape. "Long Island doesn't look like this." I said to him, "Oh, yes, it sure does. And I'm here to tell you, it always will."

1200

FORSAC

SILS
MARCH 29

FURTSCHELLAS

GENE ON THE MOUNTAIN
WRITING.

MOUNTAINS AND VALLEYS

As of late, I find myself proud of my Jewish heritage. Not the tallit-wrapped, bar-mitzvah boy pride, not the *davening*, not even the holidays, which I often artfully dodge, but more the comfort in being an outsider who sets his own rules, who marvels at the accomplishments of the Jews and how they have been able to live and flourish against all odds.

I never thought about being Jewish while growing up in Passaic, a small city with a healthy Jewish population. I didn't hit the anti-Semitic wall until I went to college and pledged the ultra-Protestant Sigma Chi and was told I belonged off campus in a Jewish section of town when they realized I was circumcised. Once those rules were set, I spent the rest of my life comfortably in my skin. The fact that I lived in New York, a glorious multi-racial city, and was surrounded by art and the people that made that art, was a big help. Every so often, I am rattled by how far we haven't come, but it makes me feel more secure in my liberal beliefs and, if anything, prouder of my way of life.

The moment when I landed on the shores of the European continent, just after it had been drowned in the blood of the Second World War, when six million Jews perished, I found myself suddenly stationed close to the migratory roots of my extended family from middle Europe. I was sent there as a lonely private, a solider who had never seen a mountain taller than Eagle Rock in Paterson, New Jersey. Cincinnati, my college town, was built on seven hills like Rome, but a hill does not a mountain make. So, when I first caught sight of those Bavarian alpine peaks, I was hooked.

Virgo is an earth sign and I've lived surrounded by water. Both my ascendant and moon, Cancer and Scorpio, are water signs. The way those mountains caressed the towns that touched them, the way the pine forests climbed those jagged slopes, the sound of farmers moving their animals up and down those fertile fields. Oh, this earth sign was hooked. This lonely private, soon to be corporal, lecturing new arrivals at the Repo Depot, was falling into the cadence of the German language and at the same time easing into the arms of homosexuality. Even my trip to Dachau, horrific as it was, didn't stop me from falling in love with European living. I've been back to the mountains many times after I was discharged, always with Gene, and often with my cousin Lloyd and his wife, Roz.

Eight countries claim the Alps. If you look at three-dimensional maps of this wondrous region, it is almost impossible to know if you are in Switzerland or Germany, France or Italy, or the Austrian or Italian Tyrol. I have seen hidden gems like Merano in the German-speaking section of Italy, played tennis 6,000 feet above the valley that snakes its way to the high mountains of Innsbruck, and the beauty of Asolo at the foothills of the Dolomites, which for me are the most beautiful mountains of all, with

OPPOSITE The height of vacationing decadence: Gene writing in his journal a mile high above the Swiss Engadin Valley, sipping Gluhwein, and completely unaware that I was sketching him into my life.

OVERLEAF This double portrait perfectly frames our love of mountains —mountains that seem to represent a life well-lived far from the valleys of reality.

PAGES 272–273 Quick strokes that "make a mountain," hiking down the Val Fex, a valley that I believe is the most beautiful in all of Switzerland.

VAL FEX   MARCH 29 -   FI

GRAND HOTEL DUCHI d Aosta
TRIESTE APRIL 15 2146

TRIESTE

their red, jagged peaks, poking the low-lying cloud cover. The Hotel Villa Cipriani there is where Gene and I spent New Year's Eve with Roz and Lloyd, while they danced the champagne night away. Gene and I were frustrated that we had to hold hands under the table, but the sex was great when we got back to our room. There's the great, winding Maloja Pass between two of our favorite hotels, the Villa Serbelloni in Bellagio on Lake Como and the Waldhaus in Sils Maria, Switzerland. Como has its Villa D'Este, but for us, it was always the more spartan, and if anything more elegant Serbiloni, although they had terribly unkempt tennis courts.

The Waldhaus that sits frozen over the three lakes that make up the St. Moritz valley is possibly my favorite hotel. All of the Swiss amenities are there for your pleasure, rooms that tilt over the valley and glow with the winter sun, a cocktail hour often attended by guests with their well-behaved dogs. That is where I first fell in love with standard poodles. There were aging musicians playing Schubert and Lehar until dinner was served, and perhaps the most beautiful ride down the Backwoods of Fex Valley, in the hotel's Gelandewagen.

And of course, there are the lakes—Como, Lugano, Maggiore, Garda—for me, the crown jewels of Italy, all fringed with Alpine peaks and aging postcard towns. There are the great cities that throb with operatic overtones like Munich, Geneva, Milan, and my favorite, Zurich, with its glorious Hotel Bauer Au Lac and Gustav Zumsteg's artsy restaurant. On Austria's eastern edge are the softer slopes around Salzburg and its Mozart chocolate factory. Then, of course, Vienna, where my father set off from in 1920 to find his life in America. Until his death, my father's favorite television show was the New Year's Eve concert from Vienna when Johann Strauss' *Radetsky Waltz* demands that the audience clap along with its beat. He became a little boy again. The Danube never stopped flowing for him.

On the western edge of the Alps is the full-on Italian city of Milan, Gene's favorite. Our hotel of choice was always the Grand Hotel et de Milan where Verdi stayed. I think he must have stayed in every room or at least the ones we booked. The food, the shops, the dirt, and its slightly grubby character didn't bother us at all. There was La Scala, the opera mecca where we went to the opening night performance of *Fidelio*, to see my favorite soprano and my friend, Leonie Rysanek.

The train ride along the Po Valley was spectacular, keeping an arm's length from those mountains due north, traveling through towns like Bergamo, Riva Garda, Vicenza, Verona, and then ending in the magic of Venice, which brings me full circle to Jan Morris, the 92-year-old writer from Wales, and to the city of Trieste that has captured my heart. It is a city that she writes about in her book, *Trieste and the Meaning of Nowhere*. It's a city I visited twice, both with Lloyd and Roz, sipped the Illi coffee, wandered the Adriatic wharf, been hosted by my new friend Paolo who lives there comfortably in its middle class underbelly. This was the city Gene always wanted to go to, and never did, a city that attracted James Joyce and Sigmund Freud. I've sent

OPPOSITE The writer who inspired me to sit down and write this memoir was Jan Morris and her love for Trieste, which was expressed in her book, *Trieste and the Meaning of Nowhere*, which can be seen at every turn, in every room, and on every ashtray.

OPPOSITE My sketches appear throughout this memoir—quick strokes that capture my lifestyle. This sketch was drawn sitting in the hotel lobby of my favorite Italian city, Trieste.

OVERLEAF This is city Gene always wanted to visit—Trieste, lived in by his hero, James Joyce. He never got there but I am making up for it. It is a city that can easily lull you into its charms. This picture captures its seductive magic.

other people to enjoy its pleasures, but most have not responded as much as I have. I just reread Jan's book. Maybe it's the place that keeps me linked to Gene, maybe he walks the streets with me. I went to their grubby aquarium on our first visit and was seduced by a lonely triggerfish that kept rubbing up against the glass and eyeing me as it slithered by. I stood there for a good 15 minutes, convinced that he was a messenger from Gene, telling me that it was all okay. So, Jan, my title may be, *Trieste and the Meaning of Everywhere*.

A FAMILY OF FRIENDS

On my 92nd birthday, I received a card from Jean Bakelar, my first crush from kindergarten. She was by all accounts the most beautiful Gentile in Passaic. We lived around the corner from one another and often walked home from school together. I can still see her hanks of glossy blonde hair swinging across her shoulders.

My friend, Selma, who over the years has remained a year older than me, was Brooklyn-born to a grocer's family, has flitted in and out of my life for over seven decades, a wonderful ambulance chaser with a slicing sense of humor. She was the one responsible for getting Gene back into my life and I am forever grateful. Early on, she had an affair with another friend, Edie Windsor, although Selma would say she is not a lesbian. Edie was the woman responsible for the laws that almost leveled the playing field in the gay world: the right to marry, to touch each other in plain sight, to raise children, to openly share the bounty of a relationship.

I tend to hold onto friends, as I've said before. Almost everything in my life has the mark of longevity. When do friends become family and family become friends? My brothers have never disappeared from my life and I had the most glorious love affair with my father past his 100th year. I still speak to my cousins and compare notes. There is a constant stream of friends that break bread at my house in the country.

In that stream came the Horowitz clan, which included Gene's sister, Esther, and her husband, Ben. Like juicy mussels they latched onto my life, bringing their three sons, Allan, Mark, and Evan, with them. They became the celebratory family from Passover to Thanksgiving, when they moved from the suburban grid of Levittown to the rural roads of this North Sea community. Esther and Ben's children's children still dangle from my dock.

My apartment in New York is a museum of photographs, fading snapshots of all three families, the Tannenbaums, the Hermans, and the Jacobs: my mother, Helen, dressed Kabuki style in the Catskill fields; my father astride so many horses, you would think you were at Madison Square Garden; and me sidling up against my brother, Harvey, at the 1939 World's Fair. Every family represented by a group shot, told to smile for the

OPPOSITE Two nonagenarians, my brother, Harvey and me, both with just enough breath to blow out the candles.

OVERLEAF This is just a smattering of all my friends. My father was fearful that I would be lonely in my late life. Oh "Die Vater," I wish you could be with me to hear the lively chatter of that late life.

PAGES 282–283 My annual "weenie" roast fills my deck with friendly footprints and we have the best hotdogs in town.

frustrated photographers. A few pictures of my travels give way to the sketches that line the walls. There is one picture of my 105-year-old father, toasting his 104th birthday with a glass of Royal Salute, his skin translucent, his eyes still on the prize.

Years ago, when I sat with my father and tried to explain my gay lifestyle, his greatest fear was that I would be lonely—no children, no wife, no grandchildren. Well, *die vater*, I've had my full share of family, of course, anchored by Gene Horowitz. The last 10 years, I've become attached to my brother Harvey's life. I play Herr Herman to his wife, Elaine's Frau Wesendonk. She can finish the lyrics to any song I start, even though a major stroke has limited her high notes. Their children and grandchildren have filled my rooms with their bigger-than-life personalities. My stepmother's family, the Jacobs, gave me two traveling buddies, Lloyd and Roz Siegel, whose lives are reflected on the same lake I live on.

Many of my old college friends have inhabited my extended family these past 90 years: Morty Hoppenfeld, Hoppy for short, my roommate in college who quickly became a successful, socially conscious architect, responsible for designing the perfect city—Columbia, Maryland. His ashes are there in the lake that is the core of the development. Dossie, born to be a prom queen, whose quirky take on life kept her as an outcast in Cincinnati society. She was my best friend in college. At the end of her life, she wandered around her water garden filled with frogs, waiting for her prince to come. Doctor Bill Serbin, another college buddy, stayed in my life until his late eighties. His recordings of Lily Pons singing bird-like coloratura tones at the fraternity house still ring in my ears. Born to be gay, he married, had four children, and came out in his sixties. Two opera queens that we were, his last words to me were the recognition of the passing of time when the Marschallin in *Der Rosenkavalier* sprechstimmes, *Ya Ya*. He died days later.

I've been back to Cincinnati many times, to teach and to receive an honorary degree in fine arts. I often think of the frat house and the early friendships I settled into with only men to share the shower with. I became their president and leader, my sexual desires still hidden underneath the blanket.

There were also my friends from the army, the most important being Dick Engel, who held me by the hand and drew me into the sexy world of the army underground. He was a frustrated singer with a lousy voice, who asked me to recreate our days in Venice just before he died of AIDS in Costa Rica. There was Hardy with a Texas accent that should have been recorded for posterity. He looked like the Marlboro Man with the heart of St. Francis. He should have been gay, but family life got in the way. And there was Bob Bean, the most beautiful man I ever knew, two privates finding each other in the crowded barracks of Fort Dix. We never had sex, although I'm the one that froze when he made the overture. He went on to Hollywood fame and produced a large, happy family. He may still be alive, but better I don't know.

Gene gave me the gift of Michael Mahon, a master teacher and a closet poet. He taught in Chappaqua before heading back to his home state of California to hunker down in Hemmit, the humbler side of Palm Springs. After Gene died, we held onto each other, speaking to each other almost every day. Opera talk, political talk, sexy talk, and animal talk. His life centered on his seven cats and the animal shelter where he volunteered. When he didn't answer the phone for several days, I panicked and called the police department.

When I finally got through, I was told they had just picked up his body. He had a heart attack in the shower and wasn't discovered for days. It's a horrific picture I carry with me to this very day. I made sure that the cats were taken into the shelter and he was reunited with the family he had left many years ago.

The one designer that became my closest friend in the 1960s when we were both knocking on the door to fame was Leo Narducci. Our careers ran parallel for years. He thought we were the same age, but good liar that I was, he never discovered the five-year difference until I was age outed. I believe he's writing his memoir as I write mine. We speak often, two old guys filling the telephone lines with ancient history, lovingly massaged back to life, still filling in the gaps that make our aging bones relevant. And then there is my Jewish mother, Helen Zukerman, my accountant, who has kept the IRS at bay for over 30 years.

Today, I consider the designer, Jeffrey Banks, to be one of my closest friends. He's been the most encouraging cheerleader for me to finish this book.

There are so many friends that stepped into my life after Gene, like the twins, John and James Haigney, who wore the Jesuit crown of intellect. James' encouragement prodded me to write this memoir and he has charted my horoscope for the past 40 years. The two brothers constantly fill my intellectually spare cupboard with riches. My buddy, Victor, who arrives from San Francisco every September armed with order and wisdom. He cleans the cobwebs of neglect in my closets and fills the house with operatic voices, literature, and a psychoanalyst's mind.

There is Marylou Luther, who wrote the first article ever written about me, back in the early 1960s, in which she describes me as a 'short designer' and I took her to task, asking her if she ever described Givenchy as tall and she said she did. These days, we walk arm in arm around Murray Hill. She lives around the block and is meticulously dressed in either Ralph Rucci or Geoffrey Beene. She is a reminder of all the great journalists who have written about our industry. Her birthday gifts to me are crisp dollar bills, one for every year, tied in a pretty satin bow. The bundle is now a stack. My father used to write me a check for the amount of my birthday. I stopped cashing them when he hit 70 and had the rest framed as a tribute to his generosity. He always complained that I was screwing up his bank balance, but loved it when I told him I was framing them for posterity.

There is, of course, my fashion work wife, Fern Mallis. When I interviewed her for the executive director's job at the CFDA, I told her that the job was to be a behind-the-scenes executive. She immediately said that's what she did for a living. Well, it didn't work out quite that way, and the council was the better for it. Her Aries personality won out and I quickly learned how to use her energy. Our contribution to Fashion Week couldn't have happened any other way. She now lives on my lake and I water her plants and feed the cat when asked to do so.

All of the names mentioned here that have filled my life—tennis buddies, opera buddies, neighbors in my apartment house, lake dwellers in Southampton, board members, designers, relatives, those to whom I speak on a regular basis, the hundreds I know on a first-name basis, and the hundreds whose names I've forgotten.

My father would be relieved to know that I really do have a family and they are there for me when I need them and respect my need for privacy when I don't. I believe it was the love affair with Gene that gave substance to my life, gave me the strength to continue after he was gone; but in the end, I am the one who has cultivated this family that I call my friends. I think my father would agree.

PART V: MORTALITY

There is nothing more convincing about one's mortality than the drape of skin clinging to an aging body.

FOREIGN PARTS

As I've gotten older, I find that I'm spending more time with myself. I went through a period when mirrors were my enemy. I would close my eyes when I washed my face and I made sure my sightlines were limited for fear of facing the onrushing of age. Then I began to visually separate the parts and put them together again. I would put my hand around my wrist to see if I could reach my fingertips and I never could, on my right—tennis—wrist. At one point, I made the startling discovery that my big toes were only slightly longer than the others. I was told that if the second toe was longer, you were more intelligent, and I actually believed it. The same thing about the width of your thumb on many would indicate the size of your penis. Not true.

I've always liked my feet and, believe it or not, contrary to the norm, they've gotten smaller over the years. They can swell in the heat, but there's not a bunion in sight. The moons on my nails have lost some of their crescent shape and they now chip easily, but a good manicure quickly rectifies that.

I now wear longer tennis shorts to balance my thinning legs, and long-sleeved T-shirts to hide my spindly arms, arms that bruise easily and bleed profusely when I go bump in the night.

The torso, oh, the torso that used to be my pride and joy, earned its shape early on when I became a gymnast. I could have been a contender if my high school had had a decent gym. Ours doubled as a synagogue on the weekends. That torso now quickly pulls back from its reflection. If I blink, I can see its original shape.

And then there's the face, I still enjoy looking at it. In fact, when I was younger, I have no such memories. I am pleased how well the features have fared under the wrinkles and age spots that are now hidden behind a well-trimmed beard. I have a hard time with the trimmer, so I get those runaway hairs with my trusty scissors. I've been lucky to have retained enough hair on my head to avoid being described as balding, although I'm sure from certain vantage points I may not make the cut. But I do like the silver, almost-snow color that it has become, and still comb it straight back confidently.

I use more anti-aging products than I ever did when I was young, but nothing can help revive the plump perkiness that is wasted on youth. My skin now falls like an Austrian curtain and has kept me from deep-water swimming. There's not enough fat there to keep me from sinking.

And, of course, there is the penis. It's still there, not quite as demanding, but it refuses to be forgotten. When you grow older, alone, your private self becomes your closest friend. I talk to me every day. I sing to me, cook for me and dress for me. My brother Harvey says I'm very vain. I don't think vanity has anything to do with it. There is just so little of me left to pamper, why shouldn't I treat myself well?

PAGE 290 A summer portrait on the deck that anchors my life.

PREVIOUS PAGES Like father, like son —my biggest booster at the end of my CFDA presidency.

OPPOSITE They don't stop the aging, but they make me feel pampered and prepared for the day ahead.

SCAR

I hate how skinny my legs look. What was once a shape is now shapeless. These days I've developed the habit, when seated, of crossing one leg over the other, and jiggling my toes to keep the circulation flowing. I am probably influenced by the title of this memoir, *Uncross Your Legs*. Truth is, there's not enough muscle left to hinder the crossover, and I hope that by the end of the book they are uncrossed and the circulation flows freely.

There is a scar on my left knee that has remained with me since I was about six. I was in the bathtub with my cousin Tibby at my Aunt Bertha's house. I often stayed there when my mother, who had a heart condition, wasn't feeling well. We were filling glass bottles with water and dousing each other when one of them broke and left a gash on my left knee, blood spurting everywhere. My aunt, who had a high-maintenance personality to begin with, went ballistic. "What would your mother think? We can't tell her. It will kill her." So we didn't tell her and she was told I had a cold and couldn't go home until my temperature went down.

There should have been stitches. It was a gruesome gash and it took almost a month to heal, big enough that when I cross my legs, it still faces me with anger. There are other bruises on this aging body. The other night I tripped on a stone while carrying a bottle of champagne as a gift when I went to a friend's house. And every time I rub up against a sharp surface, my skin peels away like a sheet of Kleenex. I have lost tone in my skin and all the subcutaneous fat that made me a good swimmer is gone, but that scar remains.

While writing this, I got a call from my brother, Mitchell. He and his wife Katherine, who are in the process of downsizing their lives, found a packet of letters they had never seen before. It was a diary that my father had sporadically kept from 1927 to 1941. In his elegant hand, he tells of his undying love for my mother. It was written by a man who had never finished his schooling, probably never read a serious book, never even talked easily about love. But there it is, written on aging yellow lined paper, simply stunning in its four-square honesty—how he protected her and admired her, and how he made the decision with her to carry her first pregnancy to completion even though the doctors told her she would be risking her life.

So, I am here to tell the story, and that scar has always kept me focused on where I came from and where I am today.

TENNIS, ANYONE?

One of the constants in my life has been my love of tennis. In my early teens, I belted abused balls over the sagging nets along the railroad tracks of Passaic Park. I never played on any team in high school or college, but I had an old wooden racquet that dried up after I left home for good. The University of Cincinnati had a great team, especially notable since it was a city school, not one of the more pedigreed universities in the country. Tony Trabert was their star, and people who followed tennis will still remember his name. He recently died, at the age of 90.

Maybe it was all those beckoning Hampton tennis clubs that got us, but Gene and I fell in love with this sport at the same time and I recommend it to any couple that has a good set of legs and really like being with each other. It's a sport that seems to lay bare the personality of the players. Gene was not a natural, but an ardent student. I was the natural, who never listened to the pro. I must have spent hundreds of thousands of dollars not listening. Gene's strokes were graceful with no put-away shot. I never got a real topspin backhand, but had a wicked chop shot that drove him crazy. He held onto the base line, and I was up at the net before he got his racquet back. When we played singles, I would wear him down with my strategy, but we still loved playing together. Eventually, doubles became our game. We were like Laurel and Hardy. Does anybody remember them? One of our first doubles matches was with Terrence McNally and Dominic Cuskern, his partner at the time. One morning Terrence brought his mother and father to watch us. He never took the game seriously with his Bel Canto strokes. When we finished, his mother, already sloshed, said, "My son was never much of an athlete. He plays such a sissy game." Oh, *Die Mutter*, Siegfried sings.

Gene and I were taking lessons until he died. After a long and shaky mourning period, I continued those lessons, finally listening, but still have no real backhand. Gene's nephew, Mark, often played with me, testing that backhand, and eventually, my great buddy, the artist Jim McMullan became both partner and opponent. He had the strokes and the ability to compete, but the same difficulty that Gene had to finish and win. Tennis is a psychological game, but there also has to be brute abandon when called for. That's why I like Djokovic more than Federer. My longtime friend, Carla Rich, who was the daughter of my first boss, Sylvan Rich, had strokes that I would die for, in her eighties. She listens when taught.

There was a moment when our fashion world's most famous designer–tennis player, Mary McFadden, took me to task and asked me to hit with her at seven in the morning. Washed clean of makeup, her pale skin holding onto a headband that exposed her very high forehead, she pinned me into the corner, blasting away at my anemic backhand. After an hour, she said, "Come back when you get the backhand right." To this very day, she asks if I ever got one. *It's coming, it's coming.*

OPPOSITE I've lost a few steps and my reactions can be suspect, but I'm still good at the net. These days, I often see people finger pointing in my direction, age-outing this almost-95-year-old gentleman who never developed a back hand topspin.

OVERLEAF Sometimes I could use a racquet that big. But this one's relegated to my apartment in New York, surrounded by cherished photographs of family and friends.

PAGES 302–303 This poster by my good friend, James McMullan, who I believe is the Toulouse-Lautrec of our time, quickly and eloquently captures the elegance of the game of tennis.

And in my fantasy, the person I would love playing doubles with is Anna Wintour. Her racket is legendary. I know she hits at midtown every morning and I'm told she is quite good. I bet we would make a great doubles team. I can just hear her saying, in her famous British accent, "Stan, you should have gotten that shot. It was to your backhand."

I am now still playing in my nineties. If anything, my strokes are cleaner than they were 40 years ago. My reflexes are still good, but since my gallbladder operation, I've lost a few steps and my stamina is suspect. I look forward to Sunday mornings and our indoor games during the fall and winter with Carla, David, and whomever we choose as a fourth. I intend to play as long as these thinning thighs can support this forever-young competitor. I hear there's a 98-year-old lady playing in Central Park. Now that I'm doing the clothes for the Central Park Conservancy, I should see if she needs a partner.

A WALK IN THE PARK

Walking through this glorious city, the city that has collected so many memories and landmark moments for me, is a constant reminder of why I feel so comfortable living here, a city where the rich live ass to ass with the poor in neighborhoods that clamor for fame or anonymity, where your next-door neighbor could be your best friend or just a nameless nod. It is a city that has nourished my long career, a walking city with parks that are filled with deep-rooted trees, parks that seem to slow the pace of the day.

Is there anything more intoxicating than sitting in a city park that has been plunked into the pulsing heartbeat of Times Square, possibly the busiest intersection in the world? That's what Bryant Park is, leaf-laden with trees brushing up against the city's cement and looming skyscrapers. My mornings for the past 25 years have usually been spent, weather permitting, sitting in that park, across from the carousel, eating my breakfast and feeding the scrappiest remnants to the 40th Street sparrows.

There was one day, in particular, that I remember vividly. I was listening to a live performance of Disney on Broadway—young, eager voices singing to a sparse, but enchanted, audience on the grand lawns, sitting and watching tourists arm in arm, picking their way through foot traffic, children holding onto the iconic carousel loping horses, parents holding onto the kids who are holding onto the horses, and seeing the park attendants wearing my uniforms, designed to complement this beautiful park. Chess players, checker players, sun-seeking couples, lots of iced coffee sippers, and cell phone workers on their morning break. It was a time in the park I loved so much.

That day was special, a day that Michael, my associate, and I decided to get out of the studio and go to an art gallery. New York City presents such a rich brew of wonders

that I don't get to see often enough. We went to the Neue Gallery, which happened to be directly across from the first rooming house I had lived in on East 86th Street. I remembered the night that I met Gene and waited for the phone call in the hall that would anchor my life forever. Michael and I passed the bench where Gene sat, waiting for me to get back from my night of fucking.

Gene was the man who crashed his warm, complicated personality into my life, who led me into literature and music long before this corner became my favorite museum. That's because I love Austrian art so much. Egon Schiele slammed into my consciousness the first time I saw his work, and viewing it with Michael was an elegant experience. He kept his distance, finding his own special place, until we met in front of an object that seemed to resonate for both of us. The line for the restaurant on the first floor was short, so we waited, and my heart swelled when I saw bratwurst on the menu. Bratwurst and desserts smothered in Schlag, all while facing the leafy trees in the park. *New York, New York, what a wonderful town.*

After lunch we crossed into Central Park, bumping into a woman we hadn't seen in years. How small this city can seem. I remembered her dog's name but had forgotten hers. The further west we walked, the fuller the canopy of trees became, not a building in sight. We could have been in the Catskills or the Hudson Valley. How fitting that late in my design life I am dressing the workers of this park, the world's greatest. Their uniforms will be in shades of loden green, blending in with the change of the seasons, meticulously designed by Michael and me to function under the harshest conditions while retaining their street smarts.

We wound our way back, eventually exiting at The Plaza Hotel on Fifth Avenue. Parting ways, I walked home alone, passing the spot where a lonely gingko tree faced off against the now-defunct Lord & Taylor, a tree that was anchored by a plaque honoring Dorothy Shaver, the first female president of that store, and of any major department store, for that matter. I have passed that tree for almost a half-century. My dog, Mo, would often circle it and do his dump there. I wrote a story for the *New York Times*' Metropolitan Diary about that tree and its plaque. Immediately after it was printed, the city chopped it down, leaving an ugly gash in the earth. I've called the city twice to find out when they would replant it, but have gotten no answer. I fully intend to nudge them until I get my tree back. My walk in the park is not the same without it.

OPPOSITE What a wonder, what a park. Where else in the world can you wander from skyscrapers to giant oaks that compete for the sky?

PART VI: LAST THOUGHTS

*For me, the sense of ending is like the last bars of a Mahler lied,
when even silence has melody.*

THE RUNWAY

The masks have come off for the moment. The vaccine seems to have done its job, yet confusion still reigns. The fact that I've remained on the shores of my lake without distraction has finally brought me close to the end of this memoir, and yet, there still seem to be many untold stories rattling around this aging mind, forgotten fragments that continue to push to the surface, waiting to be remembered. Some as far back as my first pre-puberty orgasm induced by aimlessly bouncing on my Grandma Tannebaum's bed. I had no idea what had happened, but I know I wanted it to happen again. I actually broke the springs on the bed trying to reproduce the thrill.

Sitting in the darkness of the Capitol movie theater in Passaic, hoping the elderly gentleman who had groped me last week would reappear and do it again. Cunningly manipulating my high school buddies into a circle jerk that they always seemed eager to join; remembering the first party I went to in sinful New York, way down on the then-raggedy Lower East Side. It was at a party that took place in a mattress-filled basement apartment when I suddenly felt a tender probing hand on my inner thigh. It was the host's hand, not far from his wife's deep-throated laughter. Within seconds, I had cum all over myself, a shock of release that stays with me to this very day, a reaction that should have erased any thoughts of living a heterosexual life. It would be a signpost that eventually led me a few blocks north to the neighborhood known as Greenwich Village, where I caught my first glimpse of a street that proudly announced itself as Gay Street. All the beginnings of my very own runway, made up of memories that have stitched the pattern of my life in fashion into a cohesive career, a career littered with success and failure, decisive decisions and luck-of-the-draw, my choice of a profession that was good cover for my sexual orientation.

There are stories like the moment I walked away from my fur-licensing contract, repelled by the pelts hanging lifelessly on the cutter's wall. I also turned away from a very lucrative bra account with Youth Craft Charmfit when confronted by a room filled with men making decisions about how to hold up the breasts of America, and there was not a woman in the room except for the well-endowed model whose vacant stare spoke volumes. Besides, John Kloss and Rudi Gernreich had already given shape to those breasts without a wire or dart in sight. I ended 10 years actively designing uniforms for the glitzy hotels in Las Vegas—MGM Grand, New York, New York, and Paris—having refused to recommend high heels for the much-beleaguered cocktail waitresses at the Monte Carlo casino. I lost the Aris glove account to Anne Klein, whose design team had already perfected the art of licensing immediately after my design team, headed by Jan Johnson, had designed the seminal Isotoner glove, possibly the most famous glove of the past century.

My runway is littered with fun-filled stories that I gladly revive when I am interviewed, like the TWA bodysuit I designed in 1975, a stripe created by using the letters TWA with a space between each repeat. In the design process, the space disappeared and TWA became TWAT. We had to trash 37,000 yards of fabric. The serving apron for United Airlines in the mid-1980s had a kangaroo pocket covering the genital area. I forgot to put a center stitch to create two pockets, and when men wore it, the change from their drinks collected in the center. Customers were complaining that it looked like they had an erection. It was back to the drawing board in search of a stitch. I questioned the odd request from the Polish orchestra players on the shakedown cruise for the very first megaship, the Sovereign of the Seas, when we were fitting their blazers. They insisted that their sleeve length be three inches longer. When I balked, the trumpet player lifted his instrument to his lips and no bare hairy wrists were exposed to break the formality he was so proud of.

And then, of course, there was the actual runway that Mayor Lindsay gave me to show my faux fur collection at the Central Park Zoo. When the unexpected bill came for that privilege, which was the price of buying a new Bengal tiger, I pleaded poverty and ended up serving 25 glorious years on the Midtown Manhattan Community Board 5. The hats I designed for McDonald's in the 1970s were made of paper that were held together by a male and female prong. Back then, cloth hats were considered unsanitary. The Scott Paper Company had already received a huge order until, under pressure, the prongs unhinged and hats were boomeranging all over the kitchen. Those flying saucers are now collectibles. I expect to see them any day on Antiques Roadshow.

Louisville, Kentucky, was the home base for the Humana Corporation. I was asked to design the clothes for their headquarters' hospital. Encouraged by the Cotton Council, I decided to use only cotton as the base fiber. The beige and white nurses' outfit was well received, but I had designed the security and janitorial personnel in the color brown. In the 1970s, I had a thing about brown. After two washings, the brown turned a flamingo pink and that was my last hospital venture.

Some days the runway was clear for take-off, no bumps, just clear sailing, just good memories that somehow seemed to fade with time. My accomplishments are often scattered, out of reach, just like the way my lists are often written on scraps of paper. For a Virgo, my sense of order is a mess, my telephone book an abstraction of disarray, horizontal lines now slashing through the names no longer around to pamper me with love. So many people I've shared the runway with are now gone.

If I had to pinpoint the clearest runway, it would be holding onto the roots of those London plane trees in Bryant Park, going back to the many days I looked down to my studio as The Tents blossomed, holding onto my great dog, Mo, as he strained to inspect the premises and lift his leg on the disappearing trees; greeting the workmen and security guards, breaking for lunch around the waterless fountain. Those early years when the industry pulled together and supported each other, solidifying New

York's position in the global game of fashion, when *7th on Sixth* was born. In retrospect, it was perhaps my biggest contribution to the fashion world. I've had three distinct careers in fashion: ready to wear, intimate apparel, and uniforms. My roots are deep in all of them, but I believe it was my role as president of the council for those 16 years that has given me the perspective to be able to write this memoir and feel relevant on my very own runway.

GILT CHAIRS

On my 92nd birthday, my good friend Carla gave me a copy of *The Master of Us All: Balenciaga*, a beautifully written book by Mary Blume. It is the story of the master designer, the first to inspire me as a student in college. He was the mysterious Spaniard who, much like Garbo, wanted to be alone while everyone else wanted to be with him. Every page of the book brought me back 70 years to the shadowy, sepia-toned Europe of the 1940s and the newfound freedom of the 1950s. Fingering the faded pictures of his atelier, pictures of his friends and private moments, tracing the silhouettes of his extraordinary craftsmanship and the people who produced that craft, made me realize how much I wanted to be with him like everyone else. There were names like Dior, Fath, Lelong, Chanel, and Schiaparelli, the brightest stars surrounded by glamour, wealth, taste, and snobbery.

It was the moment right after World War II when designers were 'discovered' by the story-starved press and, once outed, there was no going back. Those were the years when Paris solidified its place as the cultural capital of the modern world and fashion was making a strong case for inclusivity. There were tiny gilt chairs, generously spaced for the well-behaved press corps that was watching the mannequins announce their entrance. Sightlines were blocked by the crush-gloved, well-hatted clientele choosing their wardrobe for the year. Smoke filtering the sunlight from the windows facing the cityscape all seemed so seductive to this young, Brooklyn-born, north Jersey-raised wannabe designer.

Not too many years later, I was sitting at my friend Arnold Scaasi's first show at the Pierre Hotel in New York. He was all of 22. I was sitting on a very tiny gilt chair in the last row, straining to see the models. I felt alone and completely inadequate. What was I getting myself into? Did I really have the stuff to have my own gilt chairs?

Eventually, I did get those chairs, but they were never gold. They were, however, chairs that seated a lot of important backsides. There were showroom shows, theater extravaganzas, restaurants, schoolrooms, and resort hotel shows, shows at QVC, and even shows for the pilots of United Airlines. Lots of chairs, lots of applause, and I didn't miss the gold at all.

Of course, as president of *7th on Sixth*, I probably saw a thousand shows in full cinematic color. My career, which circled outward with the explosion of fashion as big business, had a more inclusive fan base. These days, when I'm introduced, they say I've probably dressed more people than any other designer. FedEx alone has almost 300,000 employees wearing Stan Herman. And yet, I believe the seed that produced this extremely diverse career could never have happened without those seductive sepia toned pages from the 1940s, those wondrous shapes and oversized bows, those icy models staring into the distant camera, almost daring you to look like them and buy your way to Paradise. It is a far cry from the street cleaners I have dressed in New York or the pilots of three airlines, to the well-stocked boutiques I've filled at Bloomingdale's and Saks with my Mr. Mort clothing, the myriad catalogs filled with my loungewear, the multi-thousand devoted customers I have at QVC, even the Central Park workforce that will be serving that glorious park for the next decade in my uniforms.

Now, I can enjoy the privilege of looking back while still remaining relevant, trying to give some order to my disorganized preferences, realizing how little time is left and yet, not frightened by that prospect. I never needed those gilt chairs. I filled my own room and kept the sightlines clear.

My memories are not linear; they tend to be scattershot, and there may be repetitive moments in this memoir, so bear with me. I'm now the "go-to guy" when someone's death is being recorded. Rosemary Feitelberg at *Women's Wear Daily* usually phones me for a quote, or I'm asked if I know someone who knew that person to get a quote. Oh, my dear, there are very few left who go far enough back when the industry was called the "dress business" just after World War II when the few buildings on Seventh Avenue produced the bulk of the "better" market fashions. My memory has shaped this book and there are few people left to challenge me.

SNAPSHOTS

Snapshot, a word from my past, a casual photograph, usually taken by an amateur with a small hand-held camera, a click of memories, and here we go…

How many people can say that their brother had an affair with Elizabeth Taylor? Well, I can. He has now been happily married for over 60 years, and Elizabeth is long gone.

I miss the warmth and camaraderie of my sample room, especially Bobo, Susan, and Dora who artfully sewed Mr. Mort designs into the hot center of our new junior market.

Can anyone challenge my meeting a very frail Hattie Carnegie, whose royal credentials overwhelmed me? It was at a party given by my first boss, Fred Frederics. Fred was the less-talented partner of milliner Mr. John, arguably the most talented milliner at a time when hat designers were fashion royalty. Lily Daché and Sophie come to mind.

OPPOSITE Awards—it's nice to get them, and keep them in sight, especially in front of my nephew Evin Siegal's painting in my studio. But eventually they are yours only, and the rest of the world moves on.

OPPOSITE Designer Leo Narducci and I are great friends, with careers that ran parallel. We speak until this very day. I believe we are the only two left from the volatile 1960s, when America was discovering its homegrown talent.

Watching Sophie Gimbel of Saks take control of a room of power players—although these days, I keep mixing her up with Mollie Parnis, even though they are decades apart. I almost landed a television show called "The Fashion Couch." Dr. Herman playing fashion psychiatrist to some of our most famous designers. Pauline Trigère was to be my first 'patient.'

I remember measuring Ann Fogarty's 18-inch waistline when we worked together for the Kalish Organization—a waistline that launched a major career during the 1950s. That waist and her love of petticoats produced one the first licensing success stories for American designers.

The bathrobe has become my calling card. It has wrapped me in the comfort of its silhouette and aged well alongside the battalion of uniforms that still walk beside me.

Sharing an apartment with Arnold Scaasi before his famous backward name change. He used it as a design studio during the day, and I slept with the pins and the mannequins at night. I was hired by Bill Blass to do the showroom sketches for Maurice Rentner. Not long afterward, he stepped out of the backrooms most designers called home, and the label read Bill Blass.

Jealously, I watched Norman Norell hold court in the back room of Schrafft's restaurant on 45th Street, off Broadway. His court consisted of many of the designers of choice including Pembroke Squires and especially Frank Adams, but I was never asked to share their chicken pot pie and iced tea. The restaurants have gotten better in the Garment Center, but I dare you to find the spritz of an egg cream in its mandatory glass anywhere in the neighborhood.

I flirted with, and had sex, once, with the formidable Jacques Tiffeau, whose atelier on Seventh Avenue replicated the workrooms of Paris—all the sample hands and tailors wore optic white coats, and there was not a pin in sight.

I formed a strong bonding in the mid-1960s with a group of young designers: Leo Narducci, Gayle Kirkpatrick, Carol Horn, Deanna Littell, Don Simonelli, Victor Joris, Alexander Julian, and Luba Marks. They were the new stars. And their moment was the beginning of American designers bypassing the established stars of 550 Seventh Avenue, with magazines like *Mademoiselle* and *Glamour* giving them the pedestal to compete for the golden ring. Out of that came the Superstars—Donna Karan, Calvin Klein, and Ralph Lauren, who wore their rings with pride.

I watched every Wednesday the windows being changed at Lord & Taylor, a ritual that announced the arrival of American designers before any other store on the avenue. It was also the first time I had all the windows and a love note from the window dresser, Bill MacElree, in full view. Oh for those Mom-and-Pop days.

Studying the Yom Kippur high holiday service cantor wailing up to the high B-flat that would rock the synagogue, but I never got a booking at the Concord.

The world was watching Bill Blass making his last bow just as The Tents went dark and we cleared the runway for the bodies that never came from the Twin Towers.

I watched the last disastrous days of designer Charles James at the Chelsea Hotel. His tiny green rooms were next to Gene and my friend, Charles Jackson, of "Lost Weekend" fame—both outsized personalities at the end of their illustrious careers, both fighting for space and breathing room in the cramped quarters of that legendary hotel.

I watched incredulously as Carolyne Roehm threw up her arms in frustration as she left the presidency of the CFDA. That gesture opened the path to my ascendancy as president, and what was supposed to be a two-year interim tenure became 16 years.

The early success of Diane von Furstenberg, the Princess of Fashion, happened just as I was beginning my freelance design life. I was mesmerized by her tight arm-holed wrap dresses when I first saw them at I. Magnin in Chicago where I was doing a fashion show. The ladies loved them after she enlarged the fit and began wrapping the world in her volatile empire.

Single malt Scotch was my drink before the liver rebelled. The bottles now sit in a forlorn state on the bar that is still well stocked.

I graduated from the McDonald's hamburger college in Chicago. While working on their new uniform designs I got hooked on the original Big Mac, which has remained in my life to this very day. I remember asking Mr. Kroc why they didn't serve chicken. His response was that Kentucky Fried Chicken owned the market.

I have designed the FedEx uniform for over 45 years and the studio is just beginning to explore the next iteration. The challenge still gives meaning to my life.

Years ago, I made a quick trip to Hollywood to design the clothes for Paddy Chayefsky's film, *The Latent Heterosexual*. This homosexual didn't get the gig.

I am not the only one alive, as my dear friend Selma Ehrenfeld is now 96 and still ruling the world from her bedside, and my longtime lawyer, Marty Weinraub, is 97, and he remains the perfect patriarch for his colorful extended family.

After Gene died, my opera buddy became Neil Calet who could slouch even lower into his seat than I could when the singing was not to his liking.

Then there was Eleanor Lambert: The woman most people give credit for organizing American Fashion. We had a formal relationship—she never truly acknowledged my design credentials, and I never used her to further them. She was the CFDA before I became president. We eventually moved beyond her controlling embrace, but until the end of her very long life she was plotting to get control back. It's odd that to this day I am part of the few of us still honoring her birthday, clinking glasses of champagne every year. When Patricia Underwood and I are gone, who will be left?

I presented Donna Karan with my Golden Thimble Award during her second year at Parsons. She was already weaving her fashion philosophy with grand gestures and ambiguous endings, a magic touch given to few.

Kay Unger received my Parsons Thimble for her sassy pleated tennis dress. I believe she has a miniature of it in her stunning Soho loft. She is now chair emerita of the Parsons School of Design.

OPPOSITE Iman burst on the scene just as I was giving my first major loungewear show at the Circle in the Square Theatre. She twirled her way in layers of tricot, and the rest is history.

OVERLEAF These great ladies of design never lunched—they came to work. From the left: Joan Halpern, Judith Leiber, Vera Wang, and Cathy Hardwick.

The talent of a chubby, Kansas-fed Michael Vollbracht was full blown when I was his critic at Parsons. The sketches were extraordinary, the clothes almost too mature. And he was already beginning to sound like Bill Blass.

I've watched a young, sylph-like student, Jeffrey Banks, lose his lean look and gain a monumental fact-finding brain. He is a walking, talking library of fashion facts, all of which have gotten him a Special Award from the CFDA. He has been my biggest advocate for this memoir.

There was Ralph Lauren, the reigning visionary of lifestyle living whom I watched prepare himself for that role when he created his first Women's Wear collection in the early 1970s. He didn't know much about the placement of bust darts, but he took accurate aim and hit the target bulls-eye–true center when he did. It remains the same to this day.

I watched Calvin Klein, the other kid from the Bronx, grow from a skinny coat designer at 512 Seventh Avenue to the sexy hunk whose irreverent lifestyle captured the imagination of legions of followers. Simplicity was his calling card, not an easy thing to accomplish, but for me, the best kind of design. His name always winds its way around the waistband of my underwear.

Michael Kors, whom I consider to be the quintessential American designer for his classy and classic clothes; Michael introduced me when I won the CFDA Lifetime Achievement Award, and I really expected a standing ovation, although no one left their seats, rendering a generous and polite applause, instead. My dear friend, Bernadette Peters, sexily slithered across the stage singing "Fever" with special, just-for-that-night, lyrics. The only person to acknowledge my speech afterwards was Harvey Weinstein, who came running over to congratulate me.

I've always had a secret crush on Giorgio Armani. The only time I ever actually met him was at a party he gave at the Guggenheim Museum. His date for the evening was my pal Lauren Hutton, who introduced him to me. Without hesitation, he reached out, held my chin, and said something about my face in Italian to me. Later in the evening, I asked Lauren what he had said, "Oh, he thought you had a beautiful face." Be still my heart.

There are so many designers who have become my friends and colleagues over the years— Vera Wang, Carolina Herrera, Nicole Miller, Tracy Reese, Norma Kamali, Tommy Hilfiger, Reed Krakoff, Tory Burch, and Bibhu Mohapatra. I've watched their careers ebb and flow, and how nimble they have been to remain relevant in such a fickle world. Some have been schooled in fashion; others are intrinsically taste makers, like my friend Charlotte Neuville, who took her elegant design style and parlayed it into a very successful patisserie business. To me they are like the feisty sparrows beating out the pigeons for my meager breakfast in Bryant Park. They are survivors and fly to the heavens of success. Watching them over the years has been a privilege I will never take for granted. How grateful I am to be a part of them.

OPPOSITE When Kenneth Cole showed at The Tents, he brilliantly used the space as a pulpit for his political views, and I loved it.

AND I'M STILL HERE

I'm old enough to remember the very moment I shook hands with Eleanor Roosevelt at a Democratic rally in Greenwich Village; dancing with Lana Turner, who had had too much to drink and fell asleep on my shoulder; dodging David Susskind's attempt to out me on his seminal talk show, *Sons of Jewish Mothers*, a show where I got down on one knee and sang to Mel Brooks. I once slipped a black smock over Gloria Swanson's head in preparation for a hat fitting at my first job as a gopher at John Frederics. I sat on the stone-cold windowsills with Truman Capote at the Everard Baths.

I remember squinting at the five-inch screen of our first television set, a Dumont made in my hometown of Passaic, New Jersey; chopping ice for our icebox and shoveling coal in our basement every few hours to keep our house warm in the winter, my brother and I listening to our neighbor, Mrs. Madison, on our party-line phone; driving the first automatic car produced in America, the Oldsmobile Hydromatic 1941; and wearing knickers and falling socks while walking the grounds of the 1939 World's Fair while looking up at the Trillon and Perisphere; riding in my grandpa Tannenbaum's oversized Marmon touring car with the chauffeur partition, but preferring the rumble seat in my Uncle Sonny's car; eating a Charlotte Russe on Pitkin Avenue and riding the elevated Third Avenue subway, looking into the lives of all the city dwellers.

Over the years, I've luxuriated in the white linen service on almost every airline; and swiveled in the parlor cars from Penn Station to Southampton, smoking unfiltered cigarettes—Camels, Chesterfields and Lucky Strikes—just like they did in the movies. I remember passing by the old Metropolitan Opera House, plunked uncomfortably in the middle of the Garment Center, and looking up at my first apartment and its fire escape that I lived in 70 years ago in the heart of Greenwich Village, the year that I auditioned for "The Fantasticks" and was almost cast in the original production. I've walked Fifth Avenue with its nine great department stores from 34th to 59th Street: B. Altman & Company, Lord & Taylor, Russeks, Best & Company, Bonwit Teller, De Pinna, Arnold Constable, Henri Bendel, and Bergdorf Goodman. And I'm still here, as Stephen Sondheim says in "Follies," working it, trying to understand why my TV remote isn't working and how the hell do I get Netflix on. I've rediscovered my thumbs and texting. I never learned how to type. My father said, "Jews don't type."

I am learning how to scan and print my sketches, using Zoom and Skype, and playing the new party game of online living. I'm lost without backup help. As Tennessee Williams wrote, *I depend on the kindness of strangers*, but, in my case, they're friends. I'm still in amazing shape, still writing longhand, applying makeup before going on the air for QVC, walking the beaches and preparing dinners for the ribbon of houseguests who have discovered my compound during the pandemic. I've blown out enough candles to light a ballroom. My mind is clear even if my step has lost some bounce.

In fact, I had just celebrated my past 30 years on QVC driving my trusty Defender the 200 miles from Southampton to their studios in Pennsylvania. It was a marathon from midnight on, with almost six hours on camera close to selling out of the caftan that was my "Today's Special Value." Numbers that would embarrass even the big box stores.

But more importantly, I will never forget the love that surrounded me, from the hosts, the models, and the producers to the customers who called in from around the country. It was tough going with my newly diagnosed arthritic hip, which affected my mobility. But the overwhelming warmth that enveloped me kept me going. I don't know how much longer I can dance the dance, but my card is still full.

UNCROSS YOUR LEGS

Coming to the end of this memoir, I am finding it hard to let go. Not because I fear endings, but more because writing it has given me a safe haven this past year and I've enjoyed it, though this past year was one of the most complicated I've ever lived through. I had my first operation at the age of 91 and was one of the most likely candidates for infection during the pandemic. Then there was the shock of the exodus from New York, the city I so love, and transitioning to full-time living in the house that I always thought would be my final resting place.

Somehow the slower pace that nature demands has given me the time to write, to feed my ducks, stretch my living quarters to accommodate close friends and their dogs, rediscover the beaches, the farm stands, the best butcher in town, and where to get my shirts ironed.

There was a week that QVC booked me twice on their late-night prime-time shows. It was the same week I was left to my own devices with no one at the house to help me make my home a stage set. Yes, I was no longer driving down to the QVC headquarters to go on air, everything now done through Skype. Although my good friend Grant Greenberg had artfully rehearsed this aging motor moron and felt confident I could do it myself, I didn't feel confident at all. He had plugged the plug, set the lights, opened the computer, and all I had to do was press the green button and look into the camera. While waiting for my cue from the show's producer that would link me back to the world, my mind began to wander. Here I was in my tenth decade, dressed from the waist up in a four-ply navy cashmere sweater, looking into a camera that would connect me to a hundred million households in a room so private that I didn't have to wear pants at all if I didn't want to, surrounded by all of the stuff I have collected over the years, sitting next to a vase filled with searching sunflowers, and holding in my hand a lucky owl figure that I had bought in Greece. In front of me was the picture I had painted

OPPOSITE

Celebrating my 95th birthday, surrounded by friends and family, and holding a cake designed by my dear friend Charlotte Neuville. I've blown out enough candles to light a ballroom. HAPPY BIRTHDAY!

327

50 years ago of our hot-waterless shack and the 150 bird figurines I have collected, me sitting comfortably on the many window ledges of the house.

I rubbed my eyes, smudging the Kevyn Aucoin concealer cream that the lady at White's Apothecary had forced on me as a gift, little sample packets that would mask my aging dark spots. I began cruising through the years, piling up moments of pleasure and pain that these walls were familiar with, crossing my right leg over the left. I waited. Every minute seemed eternal—the green light was not yet green.

The one thought that seemed to hang in the air was just how much I loved my privacy and how I was always able to find that in the very public world of fashion. Nothing could have revealed that lifestyle better than this very moment, alone with my legs crossed, waiting to enter center stage and uncrossing my legs in front of the largest audience of my life.

My friend James Haigney, the gentleman who does my horoscope, has always told me about my moon in Scorpio being in my fifth house and how it has turned this very private Virgo into a proscenium arch queen once the camera starts to roll. This was to be a 12-minute hit, set aside for my zip-front robe, my most popular item in my arsenal of at-home loungewear. When the light went on, I uncrossed my legs, pitched my voice higher and greeted the two hosts, Leah and Shawn, with my usual abundance of energy.

We sold over 4,000 pieces in the 12 minutes, way beyond the expected goal, and I was a hero once more. At the very end of the sell, the producer said, "We need more Stan Herman on the evening shows." Oh, yes, you do.

It was midnight and this Cinderella was ready to slip out of his cashmere and wrap himself in the fluff of blankets in his bedroom. There was already a fire in the fireplace. How decadent and earthy to fall asleep to a flickering flame.

On my way upstairs, I suddenly realized that my left foot had fallen asleep from all the crossing and uncrossing. I wondered if any of those front row A-listers at the fashion shows had collapsed in pain just as I did. Has writing this memoir given me the secret to uncrossing my legs? Have the private parts of my life respected the public parts and vice versa? I wonder if Jan Morris was able to uncross her legs down there in Wales. I wonder how much longer I will be enjoying the simple action of placing one leg over the other and comfortably dangling my toes in midair. How long before both feet fall asleep?

NOV 20

SELF PORTRAIT IN JOHN

I could not have written this memoir without the rich presence of my life partner, the author Gene Horowitz. I hope he would be pleased.

This book could not have happened without every good person who has contributed to the tapestry of my long and fulfilling life, with a special nod to to my niece, Shana Kuhn Siegel, who took my longhand scrawl and brought it into the 21st century.

And my friend Jeffrey Banks, who expanded the narrative to include pictures and sketches that broadened the horizon of the memoir.

Additional thank yous go to: Logan Bellew, Antoine Bootz, Julian Cosma, Michael Datoli, Frederico Farina, Don Fisher, Bridget Foley, John and James Haigney, Harvey Herman, Jane Lahr, Fern Mallis, John Mays, Leo Narducci, Sam Shahid, Suzanne Slesin, and Susan Tannenbaum.

ENDPAPERS This is the list of the CFDA members during the 16 years I was president. Every name worthy of the honor.

BACK OF ENDPAPERS AND PAGE 1 The sketch, quickly drawn at a fashion show, inspired the title of this memoir.

PAGES 2–3 I used to be known as Mr. Wrap, but Mr. Zip has taken over and I am wealthier for it. Quick sketches dominate my approach to fashion. I can see the complete picture within seconds. The sketch has to excite my assistants enough to help them bring the look to fruition.

OPPOSITE TITLE PAGE This is my favorite portrait, sitting on

the balcony of my glorious studio, which had anchored my life for the past half-century. And so begins the journey to *Uncross my Legs*.

PAGES 6–7 My very talented brother, Harvey, created this collage for my 90th Birthday. This detail shows some of the bits and pieces that have become a life well-lived.

PAGES 8–9 My trusty pen loves this park, the original home to the *7th on Sixth* fashion shows, a park that is a constant reminder of the way nature can caress the skyscrapers that dominate life in this great city. For me, the simplicity of the park seating represents the welcoming gesture to enter and

enjoy the wonders of this oasis in the hot center of the world.

PAGES 10–11 This is the uniform that set the standard for fast food chains in the 1970s. It is one of my proudest achievements in a long list of uniform designs. It is possibly the first time the food industry understood how important a happy workforce was in branding their image. I loved working on it.

OPPOSITE CONTENTS PAGE Antonio Lopez captured this look from 1965 for the *New York Times*. I believe it is a perfect example of art meets commerce and conquers.

PAGES 14–15 My name is finally above the manufacturer's: The 1975 TWA uniform label that solidified my reputation in the airline world. Since then, I've designed for seven more airlines, and currently, JetBlue. I'm still enjoying the challenge.

PAGE 330 Acknowledging all the dedicated people who helped make the book become a reality.

OPPOSITE This is my favorite sketch, as it symbolizes all of my years in this business. It is a drawing of the dress form Pauline Trigère gifted me in the 1950s, and represents both the collapsible nature of the business and its promise of success.

PHOTOGRAPHY CREDITS Every effort has been made to locate the holders of copyright; any omissions will be corrected in future printings.

Jeffrey Banks: 177, 238-239, 267, 278, 280-281, all except 280 top left, 282-283, 284 top right and center left, 290, 294, 308, 326, 330; **Logan Bellew**: 59, 79, peanuts bag, 112, 115, 116-117, 142, 145, 151, 158, 161, 202, 205, 212, 213, 234, 264, 268, 272-273, 274, 302-303, 306, 329, back of back endpapers; **Antoine Bootz**: Opposite title page, 6-7, 60-61, 66-67, 69, 77, 86, 114, 154, 224, 252-253, 254-255, 256, 258, 261, 262-263, 300-301, 314; **Courtesy Central Park Conservancy**: 98, 99; **Courtesy Council of Fashion Designers of America (CFDA)**: 82-83, 85, 124-125, 126-127, 130-131, 134-135, 138-139, 162, 164-165, 166, 169, 170-171, 172, 178-179, 180-181, 191, 192, 194-195, 199, 215, 230, 280 top left, 289, 318, 320-321, 324, 325; **Michael Datoli**: 106, 120-121; **Kenn Duncan © Billy Rose Theatre Division, The New York Public Library for the Performing Arts**: 79, background; **Kenn Duncan © The New York Public Library for the Performing Arts**: cover, 74-75; **Fairchild Archive/Penske Media via Getty Images**: 174-175; **Courtesy Rudi Gernreich Eagle GmbH & Co.KG**: 206; **Photograph by Robert Giard©Estate of Robert Giard**: 100, 236; **John and James Haigney**: 141; **Harvey Herman Archive**: 18; **Stan Herman**: 285, 305; **Stan Herman Archive**: 10-11, 16, 21, 26-27, 28, 30, 31, 32, 35, 36, 37, 38, 41, 42, 44, 45, 47, 48-49, 52, 71, 80, 92-93, 95, 104, 105, 108-109, 110-111, 119, 146, 152, 155, 188, 196, 209, 210-211, 216-217, 244, 246-247, 248-249, 270-271, 284 bottom, 296, 305, 310 all, 334; **Steve Horn**: 64, 65; **Courtesy jetBlue**: 90-91; **Lynn Karlin/WWD/Penske Media via Getty Images**: 200-201; **Antonio Lopez and Juan Ramos. "Swing Low,"** *Fashions of the Times* / *The New York Times Magazine*, Anonymous model wearing Stan Herman for Mr. Mort, August 1965: 12; Antonio Lopez and Juan Ramos. "With Nickle Shades of Copper," Anonymous models in *Glamour* wearing Stan Herman for Mr. Mort, Berkshire, Westbury Washings and Adolfo, March 1968: 69; Antonio Lopez and Juan Ramos. "Bright Surprises," Anonymous models in *Glamour* wearing Gene Neil for Hampton East, Pendelton, Deanna Littell for Zacari, Stan Herman of Mr. Mort, August 1965: 72; **Christopher Makos**: 148-149; **Fern Mallis**: 51; **PATRICK MCMULLAN/Patrick McMullan via Getty Images**: 187; **Robert Mitra/WWD/Penske Media via Getty Images**: 136; **Leo Narducci**: 317; **David X. Prutting/Patrick McMullan via Getty Images**: 292-293; **Courtesy of the Queens Borough Public Library, Archives, Irving Solomon Photographs**: 240, 243; **Neil Rasmus / BFA.com**: 157; **Courtesy of Sandals Resorts**: 96, 97; **Walter Sanders/The LIFE Picture Collection/Shutterstock**: 184; **Lloyd Siegal**: 276-277; **Shana Siegal**: 284 top left; **Sipa USA/ Alamy Stock Photo**: 122; **Photos by Roe Sotorrio and QVC**: 218, 220-221, 223, 227, 228; **Susan Tannenbaum Archive**: 22-23; **Courtesy TWA Museum, 10 Richards Road, Kansas City, Missouri**: 14-15, 88-89; **Brian Velenchenko**: Back cover; **Women's Wear Daily**: 200-201. Illustrations by Stan Herman are ©Stan Herman: Back of front endpapers-1, 2, 3, 8-9, 59, 66-67, 76, 86, 92-93, 102, 112, 116-117, 158, 202, 205, 212, 213, 234, 264, 268, 272-273, 274, 298, 306, 329, back of back endpapers.

Publisher / Editorial director: Suzanne Slesin
Creative Director: Frederico Farina
Editorial Assistant: Julian Cosma
Copy Editor: Marion D. S. Dreyfus

ISBN: 978-1-938461-58-3
Library of Congress number: 2023911972
Printed in Spain / First Edition

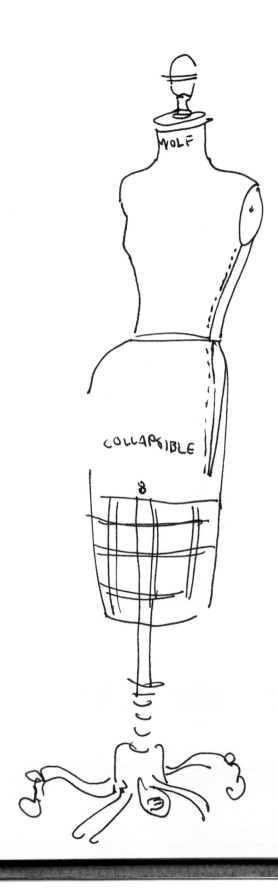

Joseph Abboud • Amsale Aberra • Reem Acra • Frank Adams • Carey Adina • Adolfo • Miguel Adrover • Adri • Akira • S
Nakard Armstrong • James Arpad • Patricia Ashley • Joseph Assatly • Richard Assatly • Bill Atkinson • Brian Atwood • B
Bantivoglio • Christina Barboglio • Jan Barboglio • Jhane Barnes • John Bartlett • Dennis Basso • Matthew Batanian • J
Bennis • Dianne Benson • Magda Berliner • Gaston Berthelot • Neil Bieff • Becky Bisoulis • Alexis Bittar • Alice Blain • F
Bouwer • Bryan Bradley • Barry Bricken • Thomas Brigance • Eleanor Brenner • Steven Brody • Donald Brooks • Thor
Capallo • Pam Capone • Albert Capraro • Victor Caraballo • Paula Carbone • David Cardona • Betty Carol • Zack Car
Chaiken • Amy Chan • Charles Chang-Lima • Natalie Chanin • Ron Chereskin • Sandy Chilewich • Malee Chompoo • J
Cohen • Anne Cole • Kenneth Cole • Liz Collins • Michael Colovos • Nicole Colovos • Sean Combs • Robert Coms
Cortazar • Francisco Costa • Victor Costa • Jeffrey Costello • Erica Courtney • James Coviello • Steven Cox • Mauree
Dartnell • Vicki Davis • Donald Deal • Maxine de la Falaise • Oscar de la Renta • Peter de Wilde • Louis Dell'Olio • P
Arthur Doucette • Henry Duarte • Randolph Duke • Henry Dunay • Stephen Dweck • Marc Ecko • Libby Edelman
Erteszek • Miss Ero • Luis Estevez • David Evins • Gene Ewing • Fabrice • Steve Fabrikant • John Fairchild • Carlos F
Elizabeth Fillmore • Eileen Fisher • Alan Flusser • Anne Fogarty • Tom Ford • Roger Forsythe • Istvan Francer • Julie J
Gardin • Eric Gaskins • Wendy Gell • Nancy Geist • Jennifer George • Geri Gerard • Jean Paul Germaine • Rudi Gernrei
Daphne Gutierrez • Jon Haggins • Bill Haire • Everett Hall • Kevan Hall • George Halley • Jeff Halmos • Halston • D
Heller • Joan Helpem • Gordon Henderson • Lazaro Hernandez • Arturo Herrera • Carolina Herrera • Tommy Hilfige
Janet Howard • Pat Iuto • Marc Jacobs • Eric Javits, Jr. • Lisa Jenks • Mr. John • Betsey Johnson • Nancy Johnson • Wini Jo
Kamali • Larry Kane • Donna Karan • Lance Karesh • Kasper • Jeanette Kastenberg • Michael Katz • Ken Kaufman • Jerr
Kim • Alexis Kirk • Kip Kirkendall • Gayle Kirkpatrick • Calvin Klein • John Kloss • Nancy Knox • Ronald Kolodzie
Lagos • Derek Lam • Isabel Lam • Eleanor Lambert • Tony Lambert • Richard Lambertson • Adrienne Landau • Kenne
Lazar • Ron Leal • Helen Lee • Soo Yung Lee • Judith Leiber • Larry Leight • Nanette Lepore • Michael Leva • Beth Le
Holly Lueders • Tina Lutz • Kerry Macbride • Bob Mackie • Marion Maged • Jeff Mahshie • Catherine Malandrino • J
Marcus • Lana Marks • Luba Marks • Jose Martin • Frank Masandrea • Leon Max • Vera Maxwell • Matthew Mazer • M
McNairy • David Meister • Jonathan Meizler • Tony Melillo • Gilles Mendel • Cecilia Metheny • Gene Meyer • B. Mi
Leon A. Mnuchin • Mark Montano • Vincent Monte-Sano • John Moore • Paul Morelli • Robert Lee Morris • Miranc
Narducci • Gela-Nash Taylor • Craig Natiello • Josie Natori • Vera Neuman • Charlotte Neuville • Rozae Nichols • Lars
Maggie Norris • Nicole Noselli • Peter Noviello • Matt Nye • Todd Oldham • Frank Olive • Sigrid Olsen • Luca Orlanc
Sylvia Pedlar • Diane Pemet • Christina Perrin • Sarah Phillips • Paloma Picasso-Lopez • Robin Piccone • Linda Platt • T
Martin Price • Lilly Pulitzer • James Purcell • Tracy Reese • William Reid • Mary Ann Restivo • Kenneth Richard • B
Rodriguez • Eddie Rodriguez • Narciso Rodriguez • Carolyne Roehm • Jackie Rogers • Alice Roi • Dominic Rompol
Miriam Ruzow • Kelly Ryan • Gloria Sachs • Jamie Sadock • Selima Salaun • George Samen • Arthur Samuels, Jr. • P
Sayres • Arnold Scaasi • Robert Schaefer • John Scher • Jordan Schlanger • Susan Sheinman • Ricky Serbin • Harriet Selv
Shupley • Tess Sholom • Joan Sibley • Helene Sidel • Kari Sigerson • Daniel Silver • Howard Silver • Elinor Simmons
Frank Smith • Willie Smith • Wynn Smith • Mark R. Snider • Maria Snyder • Peter Som • Eva Sonnino • Kate Spade
Steffe • Marieluisa Stem • Robert Stock • Dan Stoenescu • Steven Stolman • Jay Strongwater • Jill Stuart • Lynn Stuart • J
Tam • Vivienne Tam • Gustave Tassell • Rebecca Taylor • Rodney Telford • Yeohlee Teng • Marcus Teo • Gordon Thomp
Rafe Totengco • Bill Travilla • Pauline Trigère • Gil Truedsson • John Truex • Trina Turk • Mish Tworkowski • Richar
Nicholas Varney • John Varvatos • Joan Vass • Adrienne Vittadini • Michael Vollbracht • Diane von Furstenberg • Egon Vor
Cathy Waterman • Chester Weinberg • Heidi Weisel • Jon Weiser • John Weitz • Stuart Weitzman • Carla Westcott • Jo
Gary Wolkowitz • Pinky Wolmiln • Andrew Woods • Sydney Wragge • Angela Wright • Lee Wright • Sharon Wright • P